COLLECTING TOYS FOR FUN & PROFIT

William C. Ketchum, Jr.

HPBooks ®

Publisher: Rick Bailey
Editorial Director: Randy Summerlin
Editor: Jacqueline Sharkey
Art Director: Don Burton
Book Manufacture: Anthony B. Narducci
Typography: Cindy Coatsworth, Michelle Claridge
Consultant: Richard Friz

Published by HPBooks, Inc.
P.O. Box 5367
Tucson, AZ 85703
602-888-2150
ISBN: 0-89586-250-6
Library of Congress
   Catalog Card Number: 84-62580
©1985 HPBooks, Inc.
Printed in U.S.A.
1st Printing

Prepared for HPBooks by Sophia Books/Layla Productions, Inc.
Publisher: Carol Paradis
Designer: Allan Mogel

The author would like to thank the following who lent assistance
and permission to make photographs for this book:

Jay Hyams
Aaronn Ketchum
Alison Kipp
Ian Kipp
Marsha Klein
Robert Klinedist, Darien, Connecticut
Deborah Lumpe
Eric Marshall
Lloyd Ralston Toys, Fairfield, Connecticut

Special thanks to Sophie Paradis, Brice Byham, Elizabeth Byham

All photos by Chun Lai, except for the following:
Calabro Studio—cover, pages 19, 53, 59, 60 bottom, 62, 63, 64, 65.
Schecter Me Sun Lee—pages 8, 9, 11, 20 top, 32 bottom, 37 bottom, 39, 72 bottom.

COLLECTING TOYS FOR FUN & PROFIT

William C. Ketchum, Jr.

Getting Started

Toy collecting is a cherished hobby. Toys are more than interesting collectibles. They are wonderful reminders of childhood joys. Many enthusiasts collect toys similar to those they played with as children. Parents and children can enjoy toy collecting together.

WHY TOY COLLECTING IS POPULAR

Cost is one reason. Most toys are relatively inexpensive. Less popular toys, such as board games and wood toys, have comparatively low prices. Rare toys, however, may cost several thousand dollars.

Variety is another reason toy collecting is popular. So many kinds of toys are available that you may have trouble selecting a category to collect. Some people like tin toys, especially the windup or clockwork types. Others prefer the cast-iron vehicles, banks and cap guns popular during the late 19th and early 20th centuries. Many collectors seek toy soldiers, sometimes called *military miniatures*. You may like hobbyhorses, made-in-Japan robots, tops, teddy bears or trains. Something is available for everyone at every price.

A HOBBY TO LEARN FROM

When you collect toys, you collect history. You can learn about the development of transportation and firefighting equipment from toy vehicles. Most early cast-iron toy vehicles were copies of cars, wagons, trains—even dirigibles.

Toys also reflect social mores. Board games such as District Messenger Boy promote the Horatio Alger ideal that hard work leads to financial success. Miniature sewing machines and irons depict the belief that a woman's place was in the home.

THIS BOOK WILL HELP YOU

Toys have enormous appeal. However, the variety may overwhelm you at first. This book will explain every major toy category and help you fully enjoy collecting.

Identify Toys—You will learn how to identify and evaluate antique and collectible toys. You will learn how to recognize fakes and reproductions. This book includes pictures of old and modern toys. It also describes and illustrates rare and costly toys and plentiful, inexpensive toys.

Find Toys—You will learn how to find old toys. You should look at auctions, yard sales, antique shops, flea markets and antique shows. You should also search attics, barns and dumps. You never know where you may find a valuable toy!

Invest Wisely—You will learn how to invest your money effectively. This book includes tips on deciding what types of toys to buy and how many to buy. Unless you have unlimited funds and unlimited space, these are important issues.

Enjoy Collecting—You will discover how to make your collection a source of constant pleasure. Finding and acquiring toys is only part of the fun. The real joy begins after you bring the toys home. This book provides you with information about displaying and protecting your finds. You will discover ways to research the origins of your toys. You will learn how to clean and repair your purchases.

Buy and Sell Profitably—You will find information about buying and selling toys. Most antique-toy dealers started as collectors. They sold less-valuable toys as they acquired better-quality pieces. To buy and sell to your best advantage, you must understand the factors affecting prices. These include a toy's condition and location. The same toy may cost more in one part of the country than in another. It may cost more in a city than in a rural area. This book gives you price ranges for popular toys.

The business aspects of toy collecting are important. However, most of us don't collect toys to get rich. We collect them because they bring back memories. We can also share toy collecting with our children. Few hobbies offer such dividends!

Here's what many toy collectors dream about—a fine collection of late 19th- and early 20th-century cast-iron and tin toys.

Glossary

Animated toys—Spring-driven playthings named for their lifelike movements.

Automatons—Clockwork-driven figures that perform complex movements. They usually have doll-like bodies with composition or porcelain heads.

Balance wheel—On horse-drawn vehicles, a small movable or stationary wheel that facilitates movement across the floor. Balance wheels are usually attached to a front hoof or to a shaft suspended between a pair of horses.

Birmingham dribblers—English steam locomotives. Refers to puddles that formed around the engine as the steam condensed.

Board games—Games played on printed boards, or *courses.* The boards are usually marked with signals. Players' movements on the board are determined by casting dice, turning cards or spinning a wheel.

Box toys—Playthings sold or stored in wood or cardboard boxes. Well-known box toys include construction sets and chemistry sets.

Camphene—Highly explosive liquid fuel used to operate some steam trains. It was a forerunner of kerosene.

Carpet runners—Tin and cast-iron trains that did not run on tracks.

Cast iron—Iron with high carbon content. Cast iron is shaped when it is poured into a mold while in a hot, liquid state. Although brittle, cast iron is inexpensive and popular with toy manufacturers.

Clockwork—A sheet-brass and steel mechanism used to animate toys. Clockwork consists of a series of interlocking gears with teeth. These gears move as a spring uncoils.

Composition—Material used in toy making. Composition is wood or paper pulp, glue, and sawdust or plastic. It can be shaped when soft, and painted after it hardens.

Counters—Pieces moved across the surface of a board game.

Crazing—Lines that resemble spider webs running through the paint on an old toy. These lines result from age.

Die casting—A technique for making metal objects. A molten alloy is forced into a mold and pressure is maintained until the alloy has hardened.

Drive wheel—On toy locomotives, a wheel attached to a piston rod that transmits energy from a power source.

Elastoline—A type of composition material that could be molded into detailed figures.

Embossed decoration—Raised ornament produced as an object is molded. Embossed decoration is not applied separately.

Express wagon—A wagon with rail sides.

Factories—Large manufacturing plants using production lines. Also small shops that produced toys before the Civil War.

Flats—Two-dimensional lead soldiers with engraved decorations.

Floor runner—A toy designed to run on a flat surface.

Folk toys—Hand-carved wood playthings.

Friction inertia wheel—See *friction toy.*

Friction toy—A toy with a heavy cast-metal wheel mounted on a drive shaft. The shaft is connected to the wheels of the toy. As the toy is pushed forward, the cast-metal wheel, also called the *flywheel,* spins as it comes in contact with the ground. This engages the drive shaft, which turns the toy's wheels.

Gray iron—A type of iron used to make cast-iron toys.

Hollow casting—A technique for making lightweight objects. Molten lead is poured into a mold, and the mold is then quickly emptied. What remains is a hollow shell.

A bunker set with a group of German World War II soldiers made of Elastoline, a composition material.

A brightly decorated ship with wind-up airplanes.

This World War I biplane toy is powered by a friction motor.

This rowing shell is a rare cast-iron pull toy.

This unusual velocipede is made of painted, saw-cut wood.

Hollow-cast soldiers—Lead soldiers made with a thin shell of lead alloy.

Japan—A technique for decorating toys. Involves applying several layers of paint and then a coat of lacquer.

Jigsaw—A saw with a thin, flexible blade. Jigsaws are used to make intricate, often curving, cuts. During the 19th century, most wood toys were cut out with a jigsaw.

Lead soldiers—Type of toy soldier. Made with lead and lead alloys.

Lithography—A process used to decorate toys. It involves transferring an image from a flat stone or metal plate to another surface.

Mechanical bank—A bank with several moving parts.

Military miniatures—A collectors' term for toy soldiers.

Misery beasts—See *penny beasts.*

Money boxes—British term for *banks.*

Nickel plating—A technique for coating cast-iron or steel objects with molten nickel. The nickel coating retards rust.

Nodders—Another name for *nodding-head toys.*

Nodding-head toys—Human and animal figures whose heads and bodies are joined by springs or a series of wires and weights. When the figure is touched, its head moves up and down.

Nüremberg toys—Another term for *Noah's arks* and other wood toys shipped from Nüremberg.

Nüremberg ware—Wood toys made in homes and small factories in Germany and surrounding regions from the 17th through early 20th centuries.

Penny beasts—The painted, hand-carved wood figures used on Noah's arks. They usually cost a penny. Also called *misery beasts* because they took hours to make.

Penny toy—A small toy that sold for a penny. Some sold for a few cents more.

Pot metal—A light, easily cast material that is a mixture of tin and other metals. Another name for *white metal.*

Prototypes—Cast-iron toys that are reproductions of contemporary vehicles.

Puddlers—See *Birmingham dribblers.*

Pull toys—Toys mounted on wheels so they can be pushed or pulled along the floor.

Registering banks—Toys that record the amount of money placed in them.

Repros—Short for *reproductions.* Refers to modern reproductions of earlier toys.

Run—Complete set of plastic toys from one manufacturer.

Sheet metal—Very thin sheet of iron that may be covered with tin plating or painted. Metal rolled into a thin plate. Sheet metal is usually brass, steel or copper.

Soft toys—Stuffed or cloth toys.

Solids—Three-dimensional lead soldiers.

Space toys—Rocket ships, satellites, robots and similar toys made since the 1950s.

Spelter—A zinc alloy similar to pewter.

Spring-drive—A mechanism consisting of stamped-tinplate gears that move as a spring uncoils. Most spring-driven toys run for only 2 or 3 minutes.

Stationary engine—Type of steam toy in which the engine runs machinery.

Stencils—Cut paper, cardboard or metal designs or patterns used in painting decorations on toys. The stencil was placed on the toy, then paint was brushed over it. Until the development of lithographic printing, this was the fastest way to decorate toys.

Still bank—A simple box with a slot to put money through.

Tab-and-slot method—A procedure for joining parts of a lithographed tinplate toy. Small flaps on one piece are inserted into corresponding narrow openings on another and then bent to secure the connection.

Tinplate—Steel coated with tin to retard rust. Many toys were made of tinplate because it was inexpensive and easy to work with.

Traction engine—Type of steam toy in which the engine pulls things.

Trade up—To replace a damaged toy with one in better condition.

Velocipede—A 19th-century tricycle. It consisted of a cart set on a pair of rear wheels and one front wheel.

Wheel toys—Toys mounted on wheels. Most wheel toys are large enough for small children to sit on or in. They include wagons, bicycles and kiddy cars.

White metal—A lead- or tin-based alloy used to make small toys. White metal is ideal for finely detailed castings. See *pot metal*.

Space toys are very popular collectibles these days. This Japanese toy is shown with its original box.

The Story of American Toys

Understanding the history of toys and how they are made will help you as a collector. Familiarizing yourself with American toys is especially useful.

There have been toys as long as there have been children. Many ancient toys have survived and can be seen in museums. These playthings include hobby-horses from China, pull toys from Greece, clay and glass marbles from Rome. Children played with toys in ancient Egypt, too. Various playthings, including board games and pull toys, have been found in the Pharaohs' tombs.

FACTORY-MADE AND HOMEMADE TOYS

The earliest records of the American colonies refer to toys. Children at Jamestown and Plymouth had two types of playthings. These were factory- or shop-made toys, and homemade toys. Colonists brought factory-made toys from Europe. They created handmade playthings in the United States.

The term *factory-made toys* does not mean toys produced in giant factories. Until after the Civil War, most commercially made American toys were made in small shops with six or seven employees. These shops are called *factories* to distinguish their products from those made at home. Production-line toy making did not begin until the rise of large manufacturers, such as The Ives Co., after the Civil War.

Factory-made toys included musical instruments, rocking horses and hoops to roll through the streets. The skies of the new settlements were bright with kites, a Chinese invention popular in Europe since the 17th century.

Hand-carved playthings were not as sophisticated as factory-made toys. However, they are usually more endearing. They reflect the love of a father or older brother for a child. Wood was plentiful in the colonies, and many men knew how to carve. Small pull toys, sets of blocks, dolls and simple games were whittled out of pine and maple.

Factory-made and homemade toys were popular until the early 20th century. Many toy collectors special-ize in one or the other. Hand-shaped toys are often called *folk toys* and are collected by people interested in folk art. Early, rare or particularly well-formed examples may cost several thousand dollars.

POPULARITY OF FACTORY-MADE TOYS

European and American factory-made toys are more popular among collectors than homemade toys. The term *toy collecting* usually refers to acquiring factory-made playthings.

These toys are especially popular for several reasons:

1. Factory-made toys are more plentiful than homemade toys. Therefore, they are easier to find and less expensive.

2. Many collectors are familiar with factory-made toys. They played with cast-iron, tin and rubber toys made during the 1930s and 1940s.

3. Many collectors want to assemble a complete or almost complete set of a particular type of toy. The availability of toy-company catalogs from the late 19th and early 20th centuries makes this possible. Using these catalogs, one can identify many mass-produced toys. Collectors can see what is missing from their collections.

EUROPEAN AND AMERICAN MANUFACTURERS

America's toy industry lagged behind Europe's until the 1870s. Germany's toy-making industry was especially important. Germans began making toys for export in the early 17th century. By 1800, many wood and some metal toys were being made in Nüremberg.

Many European-made toys were brought to the United States. They usually were better made and less expensive than American toys. For decades, foreign competition prevented the development of a large American toy industry.

Brown and Ives—In the 1830s, a tin industry was developed in Connecticut. The tin used for pots and pans was also used for the first American tin toys. Connecticut clockmakers were toy makers, too. Such creative manufacturers as George W. Brown & Co. of Forestville, Connecticut, and Edward R. Ives of Bridgeport,

Connecticut, combined tin-making and clockmaking to produce some of the finest clockwork toys.

J. & E. Stevens Co. — German and French toy makers were competitive in the tin-toy field. However, they couldn't match American manufacturers' skill with cast-iron toys. At the end of the 1860s, soon after the Civil War, the J. & E. Stevens Co. of Cromwell, Connecticut, began making cast-iron *still banks* and *mechanical banks*. A still bank is a simple container with a slot to put

This very early cast-iron fire truck is a rare and desirable addition to any collection.

This wood rocking horse was made in the mid-19th century. It is rare and expensive.

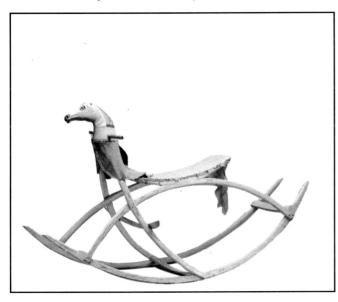

money through. A mechanical bank is more complex and may have several moving parts. The company had previously made the first cap pistols. During the 1880s, J. & E. Stevens began making metal vehicles. These became very popular and are an important category of collectible toys. Until plastics replaced cast iron after World War II, American manufacturers produced most of the world's cast-iron toys.

Weeden Manufacturing Co. — American manufacturers are famous for many kinds of toys. The Weeden Manufacturing Co. of New Bedford, Massachusetts, is well-known for miniature steam engines and attachments.

Parker and McLoughlin — Parker Bros. of Salem, Massachusetts, and McLoughlin Bros. of New York City have long been famous for board games. American toy manufacturers also excel at educational toys.

World War II had a profound effect on the toy industry in the United States and abroad. European competition vanished. Most European toy factories were converted to production of weapons and war materiel, or were destroyed. Shortages of materials forced American toy companies to drastically reduce output. Cast iron ceased to be used because it was needed for the war effort. Plastics began to replace this material. After the war, few manufacturers went back to cast iron. Plastics and pot metal were lighter and less expensive.

Battery-operated toys, which began to replace clockwork toys during the 1930s, became dominant during the 1950s. They are an interesting type of modern collectible toy.

MODERN TOYS

Europe's toy-making industry, which disappeared during World War II, re-emerged after the war. Asia began to develop an industry also. Germany and Japan, occupied by Allied forces, began making good-quality tin toys, primarily clockwork toys. These playthings are marked *Made in Occupied Germany* or *Made in Occupied Japan.* They are excellent buys for new collectors.

With the coming of the Space Age in the 1950s, rocket ships, satellites, robots and similar toys appeared. Collectors sometimes call these toys *space toys.* They are produced in the United States and abroad, primarily in Japan.

At the same time, traditional wood toys, especially those for younger children, became popular again. Wood toys from such innovative manufacturers as Creative Playthings of New York City will probably become collectors' items.

As long as there are children, there will be toys. As we have seen, toys reflect developments in the adult world. Toys and toy collecting continue to evolve. As a toy collector, you are part of an ongoing historical process.

Toy Categories

Toys can be divided into many categories. There are steam toys, tin toys, trains, games, cast-iron toys and banks. Modern collectors, dealers and museum personnel have created these classifications. Children certainly don't divide their toys into neat little groups. They just play with them!

You will find it helpful to be able to recognize different groups of toys. Even if you are interested only in a few types, you should learn to identify them all.

Categories are formed according to different criteria. Some are based on the material used for a toy. Cast-iron and tin toys are examples. Others are based on what the toy can do. Mechanical toys, whose parts can move, comprise one such category. Some categories refer to the objects the toys represent, such as trains. Others refer to the purpose the toy serves in a child's life. Educational toys are an example.

You have probably noticed that some categories overlap. Many toys fall into two or three categories. The category *trains* includes cast-iron and tin toys. Cast-iron banks frequently have movable parts and can be classified as mechanical toys.

In some cases, collectors have traditionally assigned a plaything to a specific category. For example, mechanical banks are classified as banks even though they are also mechanical toys. Tin toys often have clockwork motors and perform intricate movements, but they are classified as tin toys, not mechanical toys.

The category *mechanical toys* is usually reserved for modern toys. Most are plastic or *composition*. Composition is wood or paper pulp, glue, and sawdust or plastic. Some mechanical toys are constructed of several materials.

The system may seem confusing at first, but you will quickly become accustomed to it.

FOREIGN-MADE TOYS

As you read about various types of toys, you will notice something unusual. Many "American" toys were not made in the United States!

The United States' toy industry developed slowly. Until the end of World War I, American toy makers could not supply the number of toys American children demanded. Therefore, many foreign-made toys were imported. If a toy was owned by an American child, it may be considered *American* for collecting purposes. Don't be surprised if a toy from your grandmother's attic was made in Germany. Even today, American stores sell many toys made in other countries, such as Japan and Taiwan.

Because foreign toys have always been popular in the United States, they are included in collections of American toys. Foreign toys comprise a major part of some categories, such as tin toys and toy soldiers. However, they are only a small part of categories in which American manufacturers have excelled. These include banks and cast-iron toys.

Foreign-made examples are more important in toy collecting than any other field of collecting.

WOOD TOYS

The first toys were carved wood. Simple wood toys existed more than 2,000 years ago. Children played with such toys in ancient Rome, China and Persia. Most were dolls or small animals. Few have survived.

The first toys were one-of-a-kind objects carved by a parent for a child. However, commercial toy makers soon appeared. A man or several men made toys and sold them. This distinction between homemade toys and those made for sale still exists. The differences between these two types of toys are important for collectors.

FOLK TOYS

Toys whittled at home are often called *folk toys.* Many are considered folk sculpture. Folk-art collectors prize these toys, which are usually expensive.

One of the best-known American makers of folk carvings is Wilhelm Schimmel. He lived in Pennsylvania during the late 19th century, but had no permanent home. Schimmel wandered from one farmhouse to another, carving toy birds and animals. He exchanged his carvings for food and shelter. He probably never dreamed that his work would become famous. Today, a carved and painted pine eagle by Schimmel sells for $25,000! Pieces by Aaron Mountz, a pupil of Schimmel, are almost as expensive.

One form of folk art that was extremely popular with children in the late 19th century was the squeak

Noah's ark of painted wood with carved-wood animals made in Germany, 1850 to 1900. This 13- by 24-inch toy has a complete set of more than 40 animals, making it very valuable. It sells for $350 to $500.

Lithographed-wood Sheffield Farms delivery truck, made in the United States, 1920 to 1930. This toy is 21 inches long and costs $150 to $250. Horse-drawn milk trucks were once a common sight on city streets.

toy. This type of plaything originated in Europe, but was later made in the United States. The most notable examples were produced in Pennsylvania.

These toys were whimsical, papier-mâché figures shaped like roosters, birds, cats and dogs. They had bellows of leather or cloth. The figures were usually mounted on wood bases with coiled wire springs for legs. When pressed together, the bellows emitted a small squeak. Some bases had tiny wheels, giving the playthings the illusion of being pull toys.

Folk toys can be very beautiful. However, most toy collectors have little interest in such toys because so few examples exist. Most collectors want to buy numerous examples of the same type of plaything. Therefore, they concentrate on factory-made toys.

FACTORY-MADE TOYS

The "factories" that made wood toys were usually small shops with six or seven employees. Some carvers worked alone in their homes. They sold their products through a store or agent.

The enormous quantities of factory-made toys allow collectors to *trade up.* That is, they can replace a damaged piece with one in better condition. As with other collectors, toy enthusiasts usually seek to improve their collections.

When you first see wood toys, you may think they are homemade. Usually they are not. As early as the 17th century, European toy makers were using the most advanced machinery available to produce large numbers of almost identical toys.

NOAH'S ARKS

One popular wood toy is the Noah's ark. These box-like boats were first made during the 17th century. They have as many as 400 painted-wood figures, including humans, mammals, birds and reptiles. Looking at the tiny animals, you might think each was painstakingly carved from a different block of wood. Not so! Even during the 1600s, a piece of wood was turned on a lathe to create the rough form of an animal. The wood was then sliced vertically, like a loaf of bread, to make individual figures. Each figure was shaped with a knife.

Production of these toys became extremely specialized. One worker would paint only horses, another only cows or, perhaps, only cows with red spots on a white background. The animals range in height from a few inches to more than a foot. The people who bought them called them *penny beasts,* a reference to their usual cost. The people who spent long, dreary hours making them for low pay gave them another name: *misery beasts.*

These carved-wood animals were made until the 1930s. A few were made after World War II. They are among the most common wood playthings. Although many were used for Noah's arks, some were used for miniature farms. Others were placed in crèches or Nativity scenes.

These popular animals were made in many central European countries. A few Noah's arks and many farms were made in the United States. Others were made in England. The Chad Valley Manufacturing Co., of Harborne, England, was a major producer between the two world wars.

Until World War I, the majority of Noah's arks were made in Germany. At first the arks were assembled from figures carved on a piecework basis by peasants working at home. These toys were sold to an agent, who sold them to a wholesaler. The wholesaler assembled complete sets, then shipped them abroad. Nüremberg was the shipping center. These wood toys are often called *Nüremberg toys.*

By 1900, most wood toys were made in large factories. These establishments were fully equipped with lathes, jigsaws and the other tools for fast and efficient production.

A Noah's ark in good condition with most of its original figures may cost several hundred dollars. However, individual figures usually cost from $1 to $4. Don't be surprised if different animals are the same size. Chickens are sometimes as large as cows! Most carvers didn't care about scale. Figures 3 inches to 5 inches long were the easiest and fastest to make.

AMERICAN WOOD-TOY MANUFACTURERS

Many wood toys were brought to the United States from Europe during the 19th and 20th centuries. Many American collectors prize these foreign-made toys. However, it is easy to assemble a wood-toy collection composed entirely of American-made examples. As early as 1820, small toy factories existed in Vermont and Pennsylvania. By the late 1800s, several American manufacturers were so large that they were exporting their products.

Charles M. Crandall—A toy carrying the name of a well-known manufacturer is a valuable collectible. One famous toy maker was Charles M. Crandall of Montrose, Pennsylvania. Crandall started making toys during the 1860s and patented the first tongue-and-groove building blocks. He specialized in jointed wood figures that could hold things in their hands.

One interesting creation was the District School House. This replica of a one-room school came with desks and seats, a teacher and students, even a dunce! Crandall's toy school was very popular. You will understand why if you remember that many of our grandparents were educated in little red schoolhouses.

McLoughlin and Bliss—The McLoughlin Bros. of New York City and the R. Bliss Manufacturing Co. of Pawtucket, Rhode Island, are two important American toy makers. They produced toys from the late 19th cen-

Painted-wood horse-drawn cannon, Rich & Co., Clinton, Iowa, 1930 to 1935. Unlike most wood toys, this one has a manufacturer's mark. Marked toys are always more valuable. This plaything, 16 inches long, sells for $75 to $125.

tury well into the 20th century. Their first wood toys were hand-painted or decorated by using stencils. During the late 19th century, both companies began using *lithography,* which was faster and less expensive. Lithography involves transferring an image from a flat stone or metal plate to another surface. Lithography was used to decorate wood toys in two ways. In some cases, paper with a lithographed decoration was glued to the wood. In others, the wood itself was imprinted with a lithographed design.

W. S. Reed—Another important manufacturer of lithographed wood toys was the W. S. Reed Toy Co. of Leominster, Massachusetts. This firm produced beautiful boats, fire engines and other vehicles in the second half of the 19th century.

Albert Schoenhut—Perhaps the best-known American manufacturer of wood toys is Albert Schoenhut, who created the famous Humpty Dumpty Circus. Schoenhut started his business in Philadelphia in 1872. In 1903, he patented the figures for his circus. These figures included animals, clowns and a ringmaster. They all fit under a large cloth tent about 3 feet high and 3 feet in diameter.

These figures were assembled in a unique way that has endeared them to collectors. Each figure was jointed in several places and could be put in different positions. The figure would hold the position until moved. The lathe-turned bodies were skillfully enameled. Today, these figures still look almost new.

Schoenhut figures are very expensive. They are the "Rolls Royces" of factory-made toys. Complete circuses are rare and sell for several thousand dollars. Prices for individual figures vary. A single animal may cost $70. A rare figure, such as a ringmaster, may cost $300. The best way to collect a circus is piece by piece. About 30 figures exist. Because they were factory-made, they are compatible. A piece made in 1910 will match another made a decade later.

The early deluxe-model animal figures had glass eyes rather than painted eyes. They are more difficult to find.

Although collectors prize the Schoenhut Humpty Dumpty circuses, they are even more interested in the limited-edition Teddy Roosevelt and his African Safari. Roosevelt and some of the animals can cost $800 to $1,000 apiece. The rarest animal figure is probably the gorilla, which can cost more than $1,000.

Other valuable Schoenhut figures are the early examples with bisque heads, and comic-strip characters such as Maggie and Jiggs, Barney Google and Spark Plug. Schoenhut was also a major manufacturer of toy pianos and dolls.

In the early 1950s, a firm named Delvan, of Seneca Falls, New York, began reproducing small versions of the Schoenhut figures. Delvan produced only a few figures, including clowns and donkeys. Schoenhut enthusiasts are not interested in these reproductions.

TYPES OF WOOD TOYS

Collectors can find many other types of wood toys. Pull toys are very popular. These include wagons, horses and carts, ships, trains, automobiles, airplanes, animals and other objects. They are mounted on wheels or on a wheeled base. They can be pushed or pulled across the floor or ground. Some older examples are stenciled or hand-painted. Some later examples are decorated with lithographs.

Collectors can find many other types of wood toys. Pull toys are very popular. These include wagons, horses and carts, ships, trains, automobiles, airplanes, animals and other objects. They are mounted on wheels

---

BUYING AND SELLING WOOD TOYS

• Avoid toys on which the lithographed paper is torn, faded or missing. You will have difficulty reselling such toys.
• Sometimes wood toys with damaged painted decorations are good buys. A skilled artist can restore the paint. Of course, if you sell these toys, you must disclose that the decorations have been restored.

or on a wheeled base. They can be pushed or pulled across the floor or ground. Some older examples are stenciled or hand-painted. Some later examples are decorated with lithographs.

Stick-Mounted Toys—Stick-mounted, semimechanical toys are also popular. One such toy is a flat paddle with several chickens mounted on the handle. When you move the paddle back and forth, the chickens appear to peck at bits of corn. The secret to this toy is a heavy weight attached to the chickens by a string. When you move the paddle, you move the weight. This pulls the string, moving the chickens. This toy is made in the United States and Europe.

A similar toy has a monkey or a clown that appears to climb up and down the stick. These three toys are often called *folk toys*. However, most examples were and still are produced in factories.

Jack-in-the-Boxes—Another wood toy you may encounter is the jack-in-the-box. This spring-operated plaything was developed hundreds of years ago. You may also find tops, tenpins, stilts and hoops. All are collectible.

Blocks and Puzzles—Many collectors enjoy wood blocks and puzzles. These are usually decorated with lithography. Many varieties exist, so you could put together an extensive collection. Appealing sets of blocks include those with part of a large picture on one or both sides. The entire picture can be seen only when the blocks are assembled correctly. Sets of such blocks frequently cost more than $100.

MODERN WOOD TOYS

You may think that metal and plastic toys have replaced wood playthings. They haven't. The popularity of wood toys did decline during the late 19th and early 20th centuries. Tin and cast-iron playthings were all the rage during that period. However, wood toys never disappeared. They have become very popular again in recent years for several reasons:

1. They cost less to manufacture than metal toys.

2. Wood is more suitable for some toys. Cast-iron pull toys are too heavy. Tin pull toys are too fragile. Wood pull toys are just right.

3. Wood toys are usually safer than metal toys for small children. For toy collectors who are parents, this last consideration is usually the *first* consideration.

So in the late 20th century, we still make and appreciate wood toys—just as the ancient Romans did! Some wood toys today are so beautifully crafted that they become collectors' items as soon as they appear. Examples include pieces by Creative Playthings, Fisher-Price of East Aurora, New York, and some Scandinavian manufacturers.

COLLECTING WOOD TOYS

Wood playthings, especially those made after 1930,

are readily available. Because wood toys are less well-known than tin or cast-iron toys, fewer collectors are interested in them. You can find these toys at flea markets, yard sales, auctions, antique stores and second-hand stores. Don't expect to find Noah's arks in such places, however. These toys have become so popular that they usually can be found only through dealers or collectors.

Wood toys are often found in poor condition. Dampness and age cause warping. Paint peels. Lithographed paper decorations fade or peel. Remember this important rule: Don't buy a damaged piece unless you want it dearly. A toy that has lost its original lithographed decoration is almost worthless. In addition, wood toys are harder to restore than metal toys. Learn to wait. Eventually you will find the toy you want in good condition.

Tops and yo-yos are good wood toys to collect. They are usually brightly colored, small and easy to store. Because few people collect them, they are inexpensive.

Blocks and puzzles are attractive buys, but prices are increasing. In addition, pieces are often missing. This diminishes the value.

Old wood pull toys can be quite expensive. Boxed sets, such as the Crandall District School House, also bring high prices. Examples from the 1930s and later usually cost much less. Look for objects that have lasting popularity. A Mickey Mouse pull toy or a Donald Duck bus will retain its appeal.

Some contemporary wood toys will become collectibles. You should preserve these toys. Many are hardwood. They are well-crafted and decorated with sophisticated designs. Modern toys come from many places. However, most collectors want American-made examples.

Mickey Mouse and Donald Duck pull toys of wood, cardboard and plastic, Chad Valley Co., Harborne, England, 1935 to 1950. Mickey and Donald are popular collectibles. These examples, 8-1/2 inches to 9 inches high, cost $15 to $25 each.

Stuffed elf figure, Pucki, Steiff, Giengen an der Brenz, Germany, 1950 to 1960. Recent toys by Steiff will probably increase in value. Buy them now and put them away. This piece, 11 inches high, sells for $150 to $225.

SOFT TOYS

Stuffed or cloth toys are called *soft toys*. These playthings have cloth bodies and are filled with material such as sawdust or cotton batting. They are cute and cuddly.

TEDDY BEARS

The best-known, most popular soft toy is the teddy bear. Usually made of plush or wool filled with sawdust, the teddy bear originated in 1903. The story of its birth is interesting.

President Teddy Roosevelt loved to hunt. On a trip to the South, he went bear hunting. After a few hours, it looked as though the chief of state was not going to have any luck. A group of local citizens used hunting dogs to corner a bear cub. They tied the cub to a tree so Roosevelt could shoot it.

The president refused to shoot the animal in such an unsporting way. The Washington Post printed a cartoon in 1903 showing the incident. Morris Michtom, owner of the Ideal Novelty & Toy Co. of Brooklyn, New York, saw the cartoon. He asked Roosevelt for permission to make a stuffed toy bear and call it Teddy's bear. In time, the name was shortened to teddy bear.

Teddy bears became collectible immediately. By 1907, a German company, Steiff, was producing nearly 1 million examples each year. Today, many companies make teddy bears.

Knowledgeable collectors look for the teddy bears made before 1920. You can recognize these by their long, pointed noses and humped backs. Later bears usually have flat faces and pug noses.

Walking elephant, composition and cloth with clockwork motor, Roullet & Decamps, Paris, 1890 to 1905. French manufacturers produced some of the most interesting mechanical animals, including ones that appeared to eat, drink or walk. This example is 11 inches high and costs $300 to $400.

Toy Categories **17**

FACTORY-MADE SOFT TOYS

For many centuries, soft toys were among the few toys most children owned. Children in ancient Egypt and Rome played with them. However, you will not see many old stuffed toys outside museums. Collectors concentrate on those made in large factories from the late 19th century to the present.

Two types of factory-made soft toys exist. Some early examples were pieces of cotton cloth with lithographed designs. You cut out the designs and sewed them together. You had to supply your own cotton or sawdust filling.

Two American companies are known for such toys. The Arnold Print Works of North Adams, Massachusetts, is one. This company operated from about 1876 until 1919. The Art Fabric Mills of New Haven, Connecticut, is another. It operated from about 1899 to 1910. Both companies printed trademarks on their products. Many collectors are interested in these playthings because these toys are usually easy to identify.

You will be amazed at how many different toys these factories produced. Arnold Print Works made cats, dogs, lambs, a hen and chicks, horses, and donkeys. Art Fabric Mills produced beanbags and several types of cats and dogs. Both companies made soft toys to promote foods and other products. Art Fabric Mills made an unusual set of tenpins shaped like brownies.

EUROPEAN MANUFACTURERS

The most important European manufacturers included the German companies Steiff, Gebrüder Bing, and Schuco.

Steiff—The firm of Giengen an der Brenz, Germany, was established in 1893. It remains one of the world's most important toy manufacturers. Unlike American companies, Steiff produced fully developed soft toys rather than cloth patterns that could be made into toys. Over the years, Steiff has produced hundreds of different animal and human figures. All are collectible. Older Steiff pieces are more expensive than newer ones.

Stuffed Dino the Dinosaur, covered, in fur fabric, Louis Marx & Co., New York City, 1960 to 1965. Toys associated with popular television shows such as *The Flintstones* will increase in value. This example, 21 inches long, is $15 to $25.

You can spot Steiff toys made before 1920 by the seam running down the center of their faces. All Steiff toys were marked with a metal tag through the ear, but this has often been removed or lost.

Steiff toys vary in size. Some are only 2 inches to 3 inches long. Others, including ponies and baby giraffes, are life-sized.

Gebrüder Bing—This company, located in Nüremberg, is better-known for its metal toys than its soft toys. However, the company produced various soft, fur- or velvet-covered animals, including some mounted on wheels.

Schuco—This firm made amusing clockwork-powered soft toys, such as the Dancing Mouse and the Trotting Dog. One of the rarest Schuco toys depicts Charlie Chaplin dressed in boxing trunks to promote a movie titled *The Champion.*

Many different companies in the United States and Europe make soft toys today. You may find soft toys shaped like television characters such as the Flintstones, or comic-strip or movie characters. All will be collectible eventually.

COLLECTING SOFT TOYS

Soft-toy collectors usually concentrate on either one type of toy or on the products of one manufacturer. You may decide to collect only teddy bears or the products of Steiff or the Arnold Print Works. Some early teddy bears and Steiff pieces cost several hundred dollars each. Because most older soft toys show signs of wear or restoration, some collectors are not interested in them. Don't be too finicky. You should expect some damage.

Soft toys are available at antique and toy shows and at auctions. They can also be found at moving and estate sales, where their prices may be a fraction of their value. You can also find them at flea markets and yard sales. Don't be concerned about slight damage. A missing eye or gnawed ear probably resulted from a child's affection. Many soft toys were beloved sleeping companions. Once upon a time, you, too, may have refused to go to bed without your favorite bear.

BUYING AND SELLING SOFT TOYS

● Look for bears. Teddy bears, especially those made before 1940, are very popular. You can guess the age of a bear by its nose. Bears made before 1920 have long, pointed noses and humped backs.

● Teddy bears come in various sizes. To try to acquire a complete matching set—a family of bears!

● Almost any soft toy made by the German firm Steiff is a great buy. You can recognize Steiff toys made before 1920 by the seam running up the center of their faces.

● Buy examples in good condition, but remember that many soft toys were cuddled for years. Stains, tears, even leaking sawdust can be fixed. However, avoid moth-eaten woolen toys. They can't be repaired.

This charming teddy bear is a 1978 reproduction of the first teddy made by the Ideal Novelty & Toy Co. of Brooklyn, N.Y. in the early 20th century. It was a limited edition made for the 75th anniversary of the issuing of the first teddy. This toy is already worth $75 to $100.

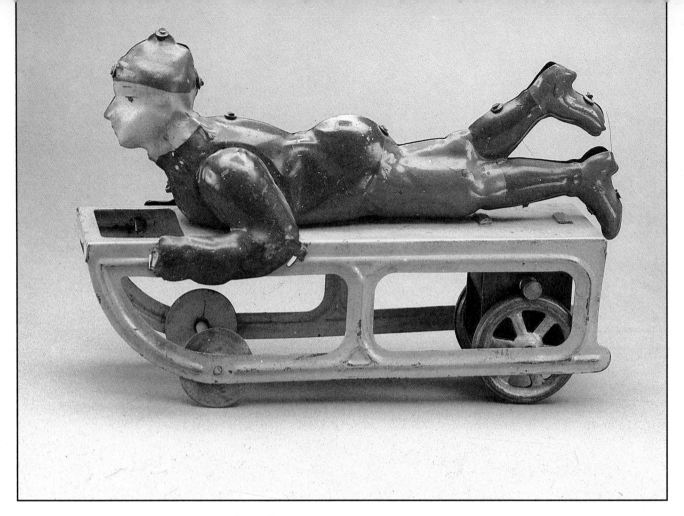

Early 19th-century painted tin toy in the form of a boy on a sled. It is worth about $45 to $60.

Lithographed and painted tin-plate Ferris wheel, Peter Doll & Co., Nüremberg, Germany, 1928 to 1938. Ferris wheels and carousels bring high prices. This toy, 15 inches high, is $700 to $900. Check for missing parts. These toys had so many parts that a few will probably be gone.

Painted tin-plate horse and cart, George W. Brown & Co., Forestville, Conn., 1858 to 1868. Brown was one of the first American tin-toy makers. His products are sought by advanced collectors. This piece, 15-1/2 inches long, is worth $250 to $500.

TIN TOYS

Tin toys are probably the easiest to find. If you look through antique shops or attend antique shows, you will find many examples. Tin toys originated in the mid-18th century and are still being made.

MAKING TIN TOYS

Tin toys usually contain other materials. Most tin toys are made of thin sheets of iron coated with a layer of tin. The tin coating helps retard rust.

Tin is a good material for toy making because it is lightweight, yet relatively sturdy. It can be easily decorated. The first tin toys produced in Germany in the 1700s were made from pieces of tin cut into specific patterns by hand. The pieces of tin were then soldered together. A faster method was used during the 1880s. Stamping machines could cut out many identical parts.

Tin toys of the 20th century are assembled a different way. Each piece has little tabs sticking up around its edges. The pieces are joined by putting them together and folding over the tabs.

DECORATING TIN TOYS

Most early tin toys have lost some paint. This is because paint does not adhere well to tin and is easily scratched off. The more paint a toy has lost, the less valuable it is.

At first, tin toys were carefully hand-painted. Manufacturers eventually found that using stencils made decorating easier. The stencils enabled workers to apply paint quickly.

Some early tin toys were *japanned*. This technique involves applying several coats of paint to a toy, then a coat of lacquer.

THE FIRST AMERICAN TIN TOYS

The first American tin toys were made during the 1830s. Most were made in Connecticut, where workers were experienced in handling tin. Connecticut was already famous for its many shops making tin pots, pans and other kitchenware.

The earliest tin toys were very simple and included items such as horns, bubble pipes, water pails and whistles. As tin toys became more popular, manufacturers made more complex examples.

George W. Brown—In 1856, George W. Brown established a tin-toy factory in Forestville, Connecticut. He made horse-drawn carts and buggies. Brightly decorated and inexpensive, Brown's toys were an immediate hit. Today, a Brown horse and buggy in good condition brings several hundred dollars at auction. Brown's firm also produced firefighting apparatus, including horse-drawn pumpers and ladder wagons.

Lithographed tin-plate toy, The Little Red Hen, Baldwin Manufacturing Co., Brooklyn, N.Y., 1945 to 1955. This toy is 5 inches high and cost $35 to $45. When you turn the crank, wooden eggs fall from the hen. This plaything was a popular Easter gift.

Ives Co.—Brown made some clockwork toys, but Ives and Co. was the most important manufacturer of this type of toy. The firm was established in 1868 by Edward R. Ives in Bridgeport, Connecticut. The name was changed several times during the next 50 years. The important word to look for is *Ives.*

Ives' first partner was a clockmaker, and the firm quickly became the world's leading clockwork-toy maker. These spring-driven toys are also called *animated toys,* a term that reflects their lifelike movements. Many toys could run for an hour with a single winding.

If you are fortunate, you may find a complete, working Ives animated toy. Ives made carousels and Ferris wheels in the 1870s and 1880s. In most cases, you will have to pay dearly for such a toy. Examples in good condition have sold for more than $1,000.

IMPORTANT 19TH-CENTURY AMERICAN MANUFACTURERS

Other early tin-toy manufacturers were located in New York and Pennsylvania. Two of the most important are Althof Bergmann & Co. of New York City, and the Shepherd Hardware Co. of Buffalo, New York. Another important company was Francis, Field and Francis of Philadelphia, which may have been the first American manufacturer of tin playthings.

Althof Bergmann & Co.—This firm is especially interesting because it made the hoop toy. This toy consists of one or two figures, often a horse and rider, within a hoop. When you release the clockwork mechanism, the hoop rolls across the floor while the figure within the hoop performs tricks. Some hoop toys include a bell that rings merrily.

James Fallows & Son—Another well-known tin-toy manufacturer was the Philadelphia firm James Fallows & Son. Fallows was an inventor and designer of tin toys for C.G. Porter & Co. of Philadelphia in the 1870s. He started his own firm a decade later.

As a collector, you may find these 19th-century tin toys appealing. As a buyer, you may find them too expensive.

Condition is an important factor in determining price. These toys are old, and many were never sturdy. This is especially true of complex toys with many moving parts, such as carousels and Ferris wheels.

Tin toys are usually missing some parts. Don't buy an expensive tin toy without consulting an expert to verify its authenticity and completeness.

20TH-CENTURY AMERICAN MANUFACTURERS

It is much easier to buy recently made tin toys. By 1900, many manufacturers had entered the tin-toy field. During the early 20th century, several large firms produced many extremely popular tin toys. Made of stamped, lithographed tin, these toys were mass-produced and inexpensive. Many examples have survived. Collectors can buy these toys at reasonable prices.

Ferdinand Strauss and Louis Marx were two new major manufacturers. Both worked in New York City. Strauss was known as *the toy king,* but Marx was more important.

Louis Marx & Co.—Marx went to work for Strauss as a teen-ager. By age 20, Marx was a director of the firm. A few years later he opened his own factory. Marx eventually owned six factories in the United States and had a controlling interest in firms in seven other countries.

Marx was successful because he recognized that the toy market was changing. During the 19th and early 20th centuries most tin toys were impersonal. Manufacturers made vehicles, machines and other inanimate objects. By the 1920s, when Marx opened his first factory, the cult of personality was emerging. Newspapers were printing comic strips with characters such as Popeye and Barney Google. Radio and motion pictures featured characters such as Charlie McCarthy, Donald Duck and Mickey Mouse.

These personalities were becoming household names. However, most toy manufacturers paid no attention to the public's interest. Marx knew better. Instead of making more anonymous horse riders, buggy drivers and carousel figures, he produced these well-known characters. His toys included the great names of stage, screen, radio and comic strips.

Marx's company made many versions of these

famous characters. The firm made so many different Popeye figures that you could assemble a collection of these alone. They include Popeye pushing a wheelbarrow, dancing, walking and carrying a parrot.

At first, collectors didn't pay too much attention to Marx toys. As a result, they were inexpensive. Today collectors avidly seek these playthings. A choice example, such as the Merrymakers mouse orchestra made during the 1920s, brings a very high price.

Julius Chein Manufacturing Co.—Other popular tin toys were made by the Julius Chein Manufacturing Co. of Harrison, New Jersey. This firm made two versions of Popeye punching a bag.

Hoge Manufacturing Co.—The rarest Popeye toy, Popeye in a rowboat, was produced by the Hoge Manufacturing Co. of New York City. This plaything sells for $1,200 to $1,500.

Tin toys are still manufactured in the United States. Most are not yet collectible. Most collectors are not interested in examples made after 1940. However, a company occasionally produces an interesting new tin toy. Alert collectors purchase these toys because they usually are excellent investments.

FOREIGN-MADE TIN TOYS

European and Japanese tin toys are collected by many Americans and can bring extremely high prices.

German Toys—German manufacturers were making tin dollhouse furniture in the 18th century. They did not begin to make tin vehicles until the 1860s. However, once they entered the field, these companies produced very fine toys, which were sold throughout the world.

Painted tin-plate battleship pull toy with friction motor, Schieble Toy & Novelty Co., Dayton, Ohio, 1920 to 1925. This piece, which costs $125 to $150, is part of the Hillclimber series of rugged friction toys produced by Schieble during the 1920s. It is 19 inches long.

German toy makers marketed their products aggressively. They designed their toys to appeal to foreign markets. They made toy replicas of vehicles that had just appeared on the market in other countries. If a new American ship was popular, the Germans made a toy model that was exported to the United States.

German manufacturers also made standard vehicles and decorated them with the flags and names of different countries. The same battleship might have an American, English or French flag, depending on where the toy was to be sold.

The years 1880 to 1910 are often called the Golden Age of German Toys. Enormous numbers of German playthings were exported to the United States during this period. In 1900 alone, one-third of the tin toys made in Germany were sent to the United States.

Marketing was one reason the Germans were so successful. Production technology was another. They pioneered mass-production techniques, using stamping and cutting machines.

You will find toys by numerous well-known German manufacturers at shows and in shops. The most important toy makers are Ernst Paul Lehmann, Märklin Bros., Schuco and Nifty.

Lehmann and Märklin are famous for their steam-

and clockwork-powered ship models, some of which have sold to collectors for more than $20,000 each!

Nifty produced the classic Toonerville Trolley and Maggie and Jiggs on roller skates during the 1920s.

The Germans made many large-scale, elaborate toys, such as flying circuses, carousels and scale models of contemporary motor vehicles. They also produced tiny, cheaply made *penny toys*. These toys were often made of tin salvaged from old food cans. They were seldom more than 3 or 4 inches long.

French manufacturers also made penny toys. Today these playthings are very popular with some collectors. Some examples sell for $200 apiece.

French and English Toys—French and English manufacturers made tin toys, but these playthings are less interesting to American collectors than German-made toys. There are exceptions. The most popular examples include candy and biscuit boxes. These boxes were shaped like houses, buses and telephone booths.

The well-made vehicles produced by Charles Rossignol of Paris and the JEP firm are also popular.

Japanese Toys—The Japanese began producing tin toys for export during World War I. German imports to the United States were embargoed, and the Japanese took advantage of the situation. These early pieces were poorly made. Japan didn't produce interesting toys until after World War II. The finest include clockwork examples marked *Made in Occupied Japan*. These were made from 1945 to 1952. Some toys from postwar Germany are marked *Made in Occupied Germany*. Both types of toys are very popular collectors' items and are rapidly increasing in value. You can sometimes find these toys at yard sales at very low prices.

The Japanese continue to make tin toys. They have been pioneers in the field of battery-powered toys, especially those relating to the Space Age. They produced rockets, robots, space stations and other unusual playthings during the 1960s and 1970s. These toys are very collectible.

You have many different kinds of tin toys to choose from. The most popular are the clockwork toys. You will also find tin playthings powered by steam, electricity, even rubber bands. Some tin toys are propelled by friction produced by a heavy flywheel. However, many popular types are not powered. Some were intended to be pushed or pulled.

The important considerations for tin toys are appearance, age and rarity. These are usually the most important factors in any area of toy collecting.

COLLECTING TIN TOYS

Because they are so popular, tin toys are usually expensive. These toys tend to hold their value and are difficult to reproduce. If you are a beginner or have limited funds, concentrate on toys made from 1920 to 1970. Prices are lower and examples are plentiful.

If you can afford older, more expensive toys, you will discover that examples in good condition rarely appear at shows. Most choice items are sold by dealers and collectors. To purchase such pieces, advertise in collectors' publications. Tin toys in their original boxes are the most expensive.

Collectible tin toys are seldom found in dumps or old barns. Dampness and water quickly destroy the metal. Don't let this diminish your enthusiasm. Occasionally, someone cleaning out an old store or house comes upon something unexpected. Opening an old box, he or she discovers toys that have been stored away for years and are in good condition. Tin toys from the 1940s and 1950s can often be found at yard sales.

Lithographed tin-plate clockwork toy, the Kiddee Cycle, made in the United States, 1920 to 1930. When the spring is released, the child pedals the bike. This toy is 9-1/2 inches high and sells for $50 to $80.

BUYING AND SELLING TIN TOYS

● Look for clockwork toys made in Germany and Japan between 1945 and 1952. These are usually marked *Made in Occupied Germany* or *Made in Occupied Japan.* They are easy to find and rapidly increasing in value.

● Before you buy a clockwork toy, make sure it works or can be easily repaired. Serious collectors pay much less for toys that don't function.

● Most 19th-century tin toys weren't marked. Examples with marks bring premium prices.

CAST-IRON TOYS

If you want to collect distinctly American toys, cast iron is the field for you. As early as the 1700s, European toy makers were using cast-iron wheels for their toys. However, European manufacturers never made complete toys from cast iron. American manufacturers did. Cast-iron toys, especially vehicles, are among the most appealing American playthings.

Cast iron is a good material for toys because it can be cast in molds. Most cast-iron toys are made from several parts. Each part is separately cast. The hot, liquid iron (usually a type called *gray iron)* is poured into a mold. It is allowed to cool a few moments. Then the mold is opened and the part is removed. The parts are fastened together with bolts or rivets.

Molds are important in toy production. Because they can be used repeatedly, molds make it possible to produce thousands of identical playthings.

DECORATING CAST-IRON TOYS

Most cast-iron toys are hand-painted or dipped in paint. Unlike tin, cast iron cannot be lithographed. Pieces of tin can be lithographed because they have flat surfaces. Pieces of cast iron cannot be lithographed because they have rough surfaces. Trying to lithograph cast iron would be like trying to print a newspaper on a piece of wadded-up newsprint!

Because they cannot be lithographed, cast-iron toys were usually painted in two or three bright colors. Red and blue were popular. Sometimes lines of gold or silver were added as accents. Cast-iron toys in these colors are very collectible.

Cast iron is so brittle that it breaks if you drop it on a hard surface. Even so, a cast-iron toy is strong and durable. Most outlasted their painted surfaces. You may find repainted examples, or examples that have lost their paint and are covered with rust. Most collectors prefer a toy with worn paint or rust to a repainted example. An increasing number of enthusiasts pride themselves on their ability to repaint cast-iron toys. These collectors try to reproduce the original paint exactly.

EARLY AMERICAN CAST-IRON TOYS

The first American cast-iron toys were made before the Civil War. These included firecracker pistols, which we now call *cap pistols.* The J. & E. Stevens Co. of Cromwell, Connecticut, was advertising such toys in 1859.

Still Banks—During the early 1860s, Stevens began making *still banks,* simple boxes with a slot to put money through. The company also made small cast-iron tools such as hammers and saws.

Mechanical Banks and Trains—During the 1870s, some American companies started producing *mechanical banks,* which had several moving parts. By 1879, cast-

Cast-iron horse-drawn trolley, the Broadway Coach, Wilkins & Kingsbury Manufacturing Co., Keene, N.H., 1890 to 1910. The earliest streetcars were horse-drawn. This 18-inch-long toy is modeled after a streetcar that formerly ran in New York City. Its value is $450 to $550.

iron trains had appeared. Banks and trains are so popular that they have become separate toy-collecting categories. They are discussed in later chapters of this book.

Wheel Toys—The most important American cast-iron toys appeared in the 1880s. These playthings were vehicles. They included horses, firefighting equipment and buggies. Trucks, automobiles, ships, airplanes and dirigibles were produced later.

Some early vehicles look very old. Don't be fooled! Cast-iron toys aren't always as old as they appear. Many were made in the 1890s or later.

Cast-iron vehicles appear older than they are for one interesting reason. When factories began making cast-iron toys, tin toys were popular. Manufacturers believed the best way to compete with tin toys was to copy them. They made molds shaped like popular tin toys. Many of these toys were quite old. A cast-iron horse and buggy made in 1890 might have been based on a tin-toy model from the 1850s. The fact that no one was driving this sort of rig in 1890 didn't matter to the toy makers.

You can be misled by the antique appearance of cast-iron toys. For example, you may find a horse-drawn circus wagon. Such wagons were used in circus parades at the turn of the century. However, the Kenton Hardware Co. of Kenton, Ohio, was producing a series of these wagons in 1952. The Kenton vehicles are the last important American-made cast-iron toys.

PROTOTYPES

Manufacturers of cast-iron toys did produce some up-to-date playthings. The most popular examples are called *prototypes*. These are reproductions of contemporary vehicles.

From 1890 until the early 1940s, manufacturers of cast-iron toys faithfully followed developments in modern transportation. Each year car manufacturers such as Ford and Pontiac put out new models. Within a short time, a cast-iron toy copy appeared. The first airplanes were duplicated in cast iron. As flying machines became more sophisticated, so did their tiny counterparts. You could build a cast-iron toy collection mirroring the development of American transportation. It would include vehicles made between the late 19th and mid-20th centuries.

FAKES AND REPRODUCTIONS

Manufacturers of cast-iron toys used standardized parts. This allowed them to produce great numbers of inexpensive playthings.

You can learn to recognize many standardized parts. If you glance at several horse-drawn vehicles, you may think they are all different. However, if you examine them more closely, you will see that they are not. The horses and drivers are often similar.

Cast-iron fire engine, Hubley Manufacturing Co., Lancaster, Pa., 1920 to 1930. This 16-inch-long toy is well-made and in good condition. It has original rubber tires and sheet-steel ladders. Loss of all or some of these parts lowers the price. This example is worth $200 to $275.

Cast-iron bell toy, Daisy, Gong Bell Manufacturing Co., East Hampton, Conn., 1890 to 1900. This toy, worth $400 to $500, is 8-1/2 inches long. These playthings have a built-in bell that rings as the toy is pulled across the floor. They are popular collectibles.

Competing companies customarily used standardized figures. Manufacturers often purchased them from factories that specialized in such figures.

Because cast-iron toys were made with interchangeable parts that were bolted together, they can be repaired more easily than most toys. Unfortunately, unscrupulous persons can use interchangeable parts from several damaged toys to make a new toy. In fact, these parts can be used to create toys that never existed.

Fakes and reproductions of cast-iron toys are a serious problem. Since World War II, interest in cast-iron toys and prices for desirable examples have increased. As a result, the number of fakes and reproductions has also increased.

Some reproductions are made from old molds owned by collectors. Others are made by creating a mold from an authentic toy. In either case, the result can often be a very good copy of the original. Many reproductions are made in Taiwan, but some are produced in the United States. Some are sold as reproductions, or *repros,* as collectors call them. However, others are offered as originals.

WHAT TO LOOK FOR

To keep from such being deceived, follow these rules:

1. If a toy is rusted, the rust should be dark brown or black. It should be hard, scaly and difficult to remove. Red-brown, powdery rust that comes off on your hand has been artificially induced. This means the toy is probably a reproduction.

2. If a toy is painted, it should show wear at the points where a child would normally hold it. These points include the areas around doors, wheels and the top of the toy. The paint may have tiny lines resembling a spider web. These are called *crazing* and result from age. Don't trust paint that is shiny and new. If paint looks as if it has been scraped away in places, the toy is probably a reproduction.

3. Be especially wary of toys offered at high prices because they are "unique" or "one of a kind." Few one-of-a-kind cast-iron toys exist. If you have any doubts, consult a knowledgeable collector or dealer. If he or she hasn't heard of the toy, it is probably a fake. It may have been assembled from parts of other toys. Don't let your desire to own something rare lead you to be deceived!

TYPES OF CAST-IRON TOYS

Many U.S. companies made cast-iron toys. The names of the most important manufacturers are worth looking for. One company popular with collectors is the Hubley Manufacturing Co. of Lancaster, Pennsylvania. Francis W. Carpenter of Port Chester, New York, is also well-known. You are already familiar with the Kenton Hardware Co. and J. & E. Stevens.

Other well-known cast-iron toy manufacturers include Dent Hardware Co. of Fullerton, Pennsylvania; Pratt & Letchworth, Buffalo, New York; and Wilkins & Kingsbury Manufacturing Co., Keene, New Hampshire.
Pull Toys—Most cast-iron toys are pull toys. Clockwork engines were rarely used in cast-iron toys because most cast-iron vehicles are too heavy to be propelled by a

Cast-iron side-wheel steamer, attributed to Dent Hardware Co., Fullerton, Pa., 1905 to 1915. Several firms made this type of steamer, which is 7-3/4 inches long and sells for $100 to $150. Steamers are popular with collectors.

windup motor. However, clockwork engines operate parts of some cast-iron vehicles. For example, such engines move aerial ladders on some cast-iron fire engines.
Friction Toys—The rarest cast-iron toys are those powered by friction motors. Few collectors are fortunate enough to possess more than one or two of these rare playthings.
Wheel Toys—Many types of cast-iron toys are available. You will find cap pistols, banks and miniature tools. You will see jacks, tops, dollhouse furniture and miniature figures. However, vehicles are the most popular cast-iron toys among collectors. Cars and horse-drawn 19th-century vehicles hold the greatest attraction. Trains and planes are also valuable.

Firefighting equipment is especially popular. Examples are plentiful. They include pumpers, hose reels, hook-and-ladder trucks, fire-patrol wagons and special wagons for the fire chief. Station houses are also available. Large pieces, such as the hook-and-ladder trucks, may be 3 feet long. These trucks are drawn by three or four pairs of matched horses.

COLLECTING CAST-IRON TOYS

Cast-iron toys made from 1925 to 1940 are easy to find and relatively inexpensive. This is especially true of figures less than 5 inches long. You can find such toys at flea markets, yard sales and at antique shops and shows. Prices for cast-iron toys have leveled off in recent years, primarily because of the increase in reproductions.

Toys made before 1925, large examples and good reproductions of popular vehicles are difficult to locate. You can find them through specialty dealers and at toy auctions and shows. Also try advertising in magazines and newsletters devoted to toy collecting.

Cast-iron Auto Express vehicle, Kenton Hardware Co., Kenton, Ohio, 1910 to 1920. This 7-inch-long piece sometimes came with a set of barrels. If they are present, the toy is worth more. This piece costs $175 to $200.

Collectible cast-iron toys can sometimes be found in old dumps and abandoned houses. Toys buried in the ground usually will have lost their paint. Remember that most toys were originally owned by children, who rarely throw away intact toys.

Even broken toys have value. They can be repaired or their parts can be used to fix similar toys. It is perfectly acceptable to repair or repaint an old toy as long as that toy remains in your collection. If you want to sell or trade the toy, you must inform potential buyers of your handiwork. Be prepared to sell a repaired or repainted toy for a fraction of the price an example in good condition would bring.

BUYING AND SELLING CAST-IRON TOYS

● Watch for fakes and reproductions. Some genuine pieces sell for $10,000, so be suspicious of any under-priced toy. New paint, new parts and restoration work may indicate a fake.

● Consult a price guide like the one in this book before selling any cast-iron plaything. Be sure you are not undervaluing your toy.

20TH-CENTURY CAST-METAL TOYS

Because tin toys and cast-iron toys are so popular, you may sometimes have difficulty finding affordable examples. In that case, you might consider collecting 20th-century cast-metal toys.

Cast-metal toys are playthings made of metal alloys. These alloys are combinations of metals, such as tin, lead and iron. They are called various names, including *white metal, spelter* and *pot metal.* You can easily recognize cast-metal toys. They have a silver or gray tone, and are more lightweight than cast-iron toys. The walls of these toys are very thin.

ENGLISH CAST-METAL TOYS

White metals were used to cast toy furniture and other objects during the late 19th century. However, these metals did not become popular until the 20th century. One of the first companies to produce large numbers of white-metal toys was Meccano of Liverpool, England. Meccano's owner, Frank Hornby, began producing the Dinky Toy line, which included many types of vehicles, in 1933.

Dinky Toys—Although they were made in England, Dinky Toys are great favorites among American collectors. They include reproductions of delivery trucks with signs for products such as Wrigley's Spearmint Gum. Meccano also made automobiles, airplanes, dirigibles and ships. Some ships were mounted on wheels so they could be pulled along the floor.

Dinky Toys come in several sizes. They range from 2 inches to 6 inches long. Good-quality examples cost $5 to $50 or more.

Two other important English manufacturers of white-metal playthings are Lesney Products, makers of the famous Matchbox series, and Corgi.

Matchbox Series—The Matchbox series includes accurate reproductions of automobiles, trucks and emergency vehicles. Reproductions of vehicles manufactured in England and the United States after World War II are especially attractive to collectors.

Corgi Toys—Corgi has made a similar line. It has also produced some remarkable facsimiles of farm machinery. Corgi's series of detailed scale models includes two sizes, the Juniors and the larger Majors.

These products are very well-made. The detail is extraordinary, and many pieces have moving parts. These toys are great favorites with young collectors. In the past decade, more adults have begun to recognize the value of these pieces. They are especially desirable because fewer white-metal toys are being produced today.

AMERICAN CAST-METAL TOYS

If you want to collect American-made toys in this category, look for vehicles produced by the Samuel Dowst Co. of Chicago. It has been making white-metal Tootsietoys for more than 40 years. Although later Tootsietoy products combine metal and plastic, pre-World War II pieces were entirely metal. Some collectors like the tiny, inch-long Tootsietoy vehicles sold in groups of five or six mounted on a piece of cardboard. The original price for such a group was 10 cents. Today, the price would be a hundred times that!

JAPANESE SPACE-AGE TOYS

Collectors are especially interested in some types of white-metal toys made in Japan. Even though most of these toys are less than 20 years old, they are becoming very valuable.

This group of playthings comprises robots and other Space-Age figures. Many were based on Japanese science-fiction television shows. Godzilla is probably the most popular toy. Others include three-headed serpents and robot warriors who fire rockets from their hands and have movable joints.

These toys are made of heavy pot metal and sometimes have plastic elements. They are well-built and well-decorated. They range from 6 inches to more than

Group of painted cast-metal Tootsietoys, Samuel Dowst Co., Chicago, 1925 to 1935. These toys range in length from 4 inches to 4-1/2 inches. The makers of Tootsietoys have produced dozens of appealing, highly collectible toys, including cars, ships and airplanes. These pieces are valued at $20 to $45 each.

12 inches high. Toys 9 inches to 12 inches high were never exported to this country in large quantities. They have always been expensive. Most originally cost $10 to $20. They will probably become important collectibles.

COLLECTING CAST-METAL TOYS

Collectors of 20th-century cast-metal playthings have no difficulty finding examples. Many pieces, such as the Tootsietoy vehicles, are still being made. You can also find these toys at yard sales and secondhand stores. Buy only examples in nearly new condition. Make certain they are complete. Try to buy toys in their original boxes. Because these toys are plentiful, they are only valuable if they are in excellent condition.

Older pieces, such as Dinky Toys made from 1933 to 1940, can be purchased from antique and toy dealers. You can sometimes find them at antique auctions. Mint-condition examples of older toys are rare.

Some cast-metal toys are easy to find. These pieces were popular when they were new. Therefore, they were made in great numbers.

Try to locate rare cast-metal pieces. Toys that never caught on with children were made in smaller quantities. They are the treasures of tomorrow.

BUYING AND SELLING 20TH-CENTURY CAST-METAL TOYS

• Try to locate a Corgi or Matchbox series catalog. Buy one of each available model. These toys will be as good as money in the bank if you keep them in their original cases with the catalog.

• Buy only undamaged toys. You can be choosy, because the playthings are easy to find. Don't try to save a few dollars by buying slightly damaged pieces or those with chipped paint. Such pieces are much less valuable than undamaged examples.

• The best buys are the large toys, such as Corgi Majors. These were made in small quantities and are more expensive.

Group of tin and white-metal toy guns, including cap guns, 1930 to 1950. Left: Clicker gun. Right: Squirt gun. Except for early cast-iron examples, cap guns are not expensive. These are valued at $12 to $28 each.

Cast-metal and plastic airplanes, 1960 to 1970. The Zero fighter plane in the center is made by Universal of Japan. The other planes are by Lesney Products of England. These toys are 3-1/2 inches to 6 inches long and sell for $2 to $6.

Sheet-steel automobiles, Wyandotte Manufacturing Co., Wyandotte, Mich., 1930 to 1938. Left: La Salle, 15 inches long, $85 to $100. Right: Coupe, 10 inches long, $35 to $45.

SHEET-METAL TOYS

Do you like big toys that work like the machines and vehicles they represent? If so, sheet-metal toys may be just the thing for you. These toys are known to collectors as *sheet-metal,* or *steel,* toys. Playthings in this category are heavy-gauge metal and are usually 2 to 3 feet long.

Most collectible sheet-metal toys are vehicles and construction equipment. Vehicles include automobiles, trucks, and emergency vehicles such as fire trucks and police vans. Construction equipment includes steam shovels, sand loaders, concrete mixers and road rollers. Few sheet-metal planes or ships exist.

TOYS THAT FUNCTION

One interesting aspect of sheet-metal toys is that they really work. Many of these reproductions function like their full-sized counterparts. When filled with sand and water, a toy cement mixer will produce something that looks like cement. The ladder on a fire truck can be cranked up and down. The hose on another fire truck sprays water as far as 20 feet. One trench digger can excavate a trench 1 inch wide and 8 inches deep!

Some vehicles are chain- or clockwork-driven. Others have battery-powered lights.

AMERICAN MANUFACTURERS

The first sheet-metal toys appeared during the 1890s. Those made during the 1920s and 1930s are the most popular with collectors. Most of the best sheet-metal toys were made in the United States.

Moline Pressed Steel Co.—The preeminent sheet-metal toy manufacturer was the Moline Pressed Steel Co. of Moline, Illinois. This company's *Buddy L* decal appears on dozens of large toy vehicles and pieces of construction equipment. Buddy L toys are valuable collectibles. A rare example in good condition may cost several hundred dollars.

Keystone Manufacturing Co.—Products made by the Keystone Manufacturing Co. of Boston are also eagerly sought by collectors.

Other Companies—Other American and some foreign manufacturers also made sheet-metal toys. The Chad Valley Manufacturing Co. of Harborne, England, produced large sheet-metal playthings from 1920 to 1940. Tonka, a Japanese firm that has dominated the field since the end of World War II, makes high-quality toys with moving parts. Wise collectors are purchasing Tonka toys as potential collectibles.

COLLECTING SHEET-METAL TOYS

Sheet-metal toys are large. Most collectors don't have room for extensive collections. If you decide to collect sheet-metal toys, you will probably have to limit your collection. You can do this by specializing. You might acquire only firefighting trucks or construction equipment.

Another reason to specialize is that such collections are more valuable than general collections.

You may find some sheet-metal toys at yard and estate sales. Most collectors find sheet-metal playthings at antique or toy shows, or through other enthusiasts.

Only a fraction of sheet-metal toys have survived. Because sheet-metal playthings were so large and took up so much room, many were thrown away.

Hook-and-ladder fire engine of painted sheet steel, Wyandotte Manufacturing Co., Wyandotte, Mich., 1945 to 1955. This toy sells for $35 to $55. Wyandotte toys, such as this 23-inch-long example, are good investments for beginning collectors.

You will have more toys to choose from if you concentrate on later examples. Tonka toys and toys made by American manufacturers after World War II are plentiful and inexpensive. If you focus on Buddy L and similar examples made from 1920 to 1930, you will encounter high prices and competition from other collectors.

Sheet-steel yellow cab with friction motor, made in the United States, 1920 to 1930. This 10-1/2-inch-long toy sells for $130 to $160. Yellow cabs, still seen in many American cities, have been reproduced by various toy makers.

BANKS

The English call them *money boxes*. We call them *banks*. Nearly everyone can recall owning one. Banks are among the first toys mentioned in historical records. One 16th-century English chronicler refers to banks "made of potters' clay wherein boyes put their money to keepe." Wood and earthenware banks were made in the United States before 1800. These early American banks are rare and do not interest most collectors.

THREE CATEGORIES OF BANKS

In the United States, collectors divide toy banks into three categories. These are *still banks, mechanical banks* and *registering banks*.

Still Banks—These comprise the oldest category. These banks are simply boxes with a slot into which money can be inserted. Some have a trap through which money can be removed. Banks without traps must be destroyed if owners want to retrieve their money.

The first still banks were wood or pottery. By the 1830s, American manufacturers were making tin-plate banks. The most popular examples were shaped like bank buildings or safes. Sometimes they were embossed or stenciled with the name of a real bank. Banks gave these playthings to children to encourage them to save money. The first cast-iron still banks appeared in the late 1860s. By 1920, examples in aluminum and white metal or pot metal were common.

Most collectible still banks were made between 1870 and 1930. These are shaped like safes, bank buildings, animals, vegetables and people. Most were painted one color, usually gold or silver. These colors were probably used to indicate the wealth that could be acquired through thrift.

Mechanical Banks—The second category of collectible metal banks is the most popular. Mechanical banks are delightful toys.

These playthings are cast iron or pot metal. They were fitted with springs and moving parts. With some

Lithographed Fishing Bears mechanical bank, made in Japan, 1950 to 1960. This toy is tin-plated and battery-powered. Like some other mechanical tin toys made after World War II, this bank is valuable. It is 5-1/2 inches high and sells for $200 to $300. You might find this bank in your attic!

Lithographed tin-plate still bank, attributed to Stevens & Brown, Cromwell, Conn., 1860 to 1870. Simple banks such as this are usually inexpensive unless the decoration is in exceptionally good condition. This toy is 4-1/2 inches high and is worth $50 to $80.

banks, the fun comes when you put the coin into the bank. With others, getting the coin in is only half the fun. Inserting the coin makes something else happen.

One popular mechanical bank is the William Tell bank. A coin placed on William Tell's crossbow is hurled by a spring into a slot in the apple on his son's head.

Toy manufacturers did not make mechanical banks until the 1870s. They were an immediate success. They were so popular that more than 1,000 types appeared before they went out of fashion during the late 1930s.

You can create a fine collection of mechanical banks, but you will have plenty of competition. Mechanical banks were among the first playthings to be collected. Enthusiasts began acquiring them during the 1920s, long before most other toys were considered collectible. Ordinary examples cost more than $50. Rare examples may cost more than $5,000. However, so many banks are available that you can amass a good collection if you are willing to spend time searching for desirable pieces.

Registering Banks—The least popular category of banks includes those designed to record the amount of money placed in them. Called *registering banks,* they are usually made of sheet metal or cast iron. Most look like a cash register and were made between 1900 and 1940. One type, the Uncle Sam 3 Coin Register bank, was patented in 1912 and is still being made. It has been continuously produced longer than any other American toy.

BANKS AND POLITICS

One reason collectors like banks is that many of these playthings are humorous. Some poke fun at individuals and groups.

A good example is a still bank shaped like a frog.

The frog's face is that of Gen. Benjamin F. Butler. A somewhat shady character, Butler was the 1884 presidential candidate of the Greenback Party. This party wanted to solve the nation's economic problems by issuing more paper money, or *greenbacks.* Butler had been involved in a financial scandal, and his campaign was not helped by the frog. It was embossed *1,000,000 for the Masses* on one arm and *Bonds and Yachts for Me* on the other. The reference to yachts arose because Butler owned a famous yacht named *America.* Butler lost the election.

Another bank ridicules William Marcy "Boss" Tweed. Tweed was head of Tammany Hall, a corrupt political group that stole millions from New York City during the 1870s. This mechanical bank is shaped like a fat man with a wide smile and an extended palm. When you put a coin in his hand, the man promptly places it in a slot in his pants pocket.

People found the Tammany Bank very amusing, and it was produced from 1874 until the late 1890s. The bank was reissued about 1905 and production continued until 1925.

One egg-shaped still bank depicted President William Howard Taft, and several banks were shaped like President Theodore Roosevelt. One mechanical bank shows Roosevelt aiming a gun at a bear. Another shows him taking aim at a lion.

Unfortunately, the humor of some mechanical banks is not harmless. Today, some of this "humor" seems far from funny and recalls a tragic period in our history. One bank is the Always Did 'Spise a Mule bank. A coin inserted in the bank makes a mule kick over a seated black figure. Both the Darktown Battery and the Dentist and Patient banks treat blacks contemptuously. Other late 19th- and early 20th-century banks ridicule Irish, Chinese and feminists.

Cast-iron mechanical bank, J. & E. Stevens Co., Cromwell, Conn., 1897 to 1905. Known as the Always Did 'Spise a Mule bank, this bank's action consists of the mule turning and kicking the seated figure when a coin is deposited. This bank is 6-1/2 inches high and costs $450 to $600.

POPULAR BANKS

Most mechanical banks appeal to people's playful nature. You put in your coins and watch what happens. You may see hunters shoot bears or ponies do tricks. Some banks have cannons that fire coins into tree trunks. Others have Santas that pour pennies down chimneys.

Various still banks and registering banks were made in England and Germany. However, almost all mechanical banks were made in the United States. The mechanical bank is a unique American contribution to the world of toys.

Many advanced collectors believe that the finest banks were made between 1880 and 1910. However, some interesting banks were produced later, when manufacturers capitalized on the interest in cartoon, radio and screen celebrities. They made banks shaped like popular characters such as Mutt and Jeff, Little Orphan Annie and Buster Brown. Many of these banks were made of cast pot metal instead of iron. Some collectors prefer iron, which is lighter. If you want to purchase iron banks, you can get good examples made between 1930 and 1940.

REPRODUCTIONS

Manufacturers have made dozens of reproductions of popular banks, including the William Tell, Darktown Battery, and Dentist and Patient. These reproductions are very accurate. To avoid buying a reproduction, follow the guidelines in the section on cast-iron toys. You should be wary whenever someone offers you a mechanical bank at a fraction of its value.

Manufacturers have made fewer reproductions of still banks. Some figural still banks, such as Uncle Sam, have been reproduced. No registering banks have been copied. Manufacturers apparently don't believe it is profitable to reproduce these banks because such playthings are inexpensive and in great supply.

IMPORTANT MANUFACTURERS

As we have seen, metal banks are an exciting field for collectors. Almost any mechanical bank has value. Look for the pieces made by important manufacturers. One leading company was J. & E. Stevens, which made the first American mechanical banks. Stevens & Brown of Cromwell, Connecticut, and Shepherd Hardware Co. of Buffalo, New York, are also important. The Grey Iron Casting Co. of Mount Joy, Pennsylvania, produced several types of reproduction mechanical banks during the 1950s.

COLLECTING BANKS

Bank collecting is popular. If you are interested in old or rare mechanical banks, you will encounter high prices. These collectibles may cost hundreds or thousands of dollars. You may have difficulty finding good examples. Check with other collectors and specialized dealers. You can sometimes obtain pieces at major toy auctions.

Still banks and registering banks are less expensive. You can find such banks at antique shops and shows, and at secondhand stores.

Still Banks—These toys are an especially good field. Except for a few unusual figural examples, they are plentiful and inexpensive. You could acquire an interesting group of banks shaped like houses. Such banks would represent various late 19th-century architectural styles. You will probably find Gothic banks and Queen Anne banks. Such pieces provide an excellent opportunity to learn about architecture.

You can also collect banks that financial institutions gave to customers as gifts. Such playthings usually carried the name of the real financial institution. Many of these institutions no longer exist.

Registering Banks—These banks are even easier to find than still banks. Most were made during the last 50 years.

Prices may surprise you. Most cast-iron still banks cost less than $50. Some interesting examples cost as little as $10. Registering banks may cost even less. Many sell for $5 to $10. You can find good examples at yard sales for $1 or less. In these times, collectibles at such appealing prices are a welcome surprise. Don't forget to deposit some of the pennies you save in the bank you buy!

BUYING AND SELLING BANKS

• If you want an interesting and inexpensive bank collection, buy still banks. With the exception of some rare examples, most cost less than $150.

• Always check the base of a mechanical bank for a rough spot. Such a spot may indicate that the manufacturer's mark has been filed off. Many legitimate reproductions have manufacturers' marks. These are often filed off by people trying to sell the pieces as originals.

• Look for modern still banks and mechanical banks made of aluminum and white-metal alloys. These are inexpensive and will appeal to future collectors.

Rocking horse made of cloth over a carved-wood body, made in the United States, 1870 to 1890. Valued as folk art, rocking horses can bring high prices. This example, 37 inches high, is worth $700 to $1,500. Rocking horses seldom bear a manufacturer's mark or name.

HOBBYHORSES AND WHEEL TOYS

Hobbyhorses and wheel toys, which include wagons and scooters, are very large playthings. You can't have an extensive collection unless you own a barn or sizable attic. Hundreds of different hobbyhorses and wheel toys exist. These playthings are delightful collectibles.

HOBBYHORSES

Hobbyhorses are among the oldest toys. The basic hobbyhorse is a horse's head mounted on a long stick. Sometimes a wheel is attached to the end of the stick. The Greeks and Romans wrote about these playthings, and hobbyhorses are pictured on 9th-century Chinese ceramics. French examples from the 1400s are illustrated in the *Book of Hours*, a medieval illustrated book of poetry and essays.

ROCKING HORSES

The rocking horse is a horse mounted on rockers or springs. These playthings are big enough for a child to ride. The "ride," of course, is the back-and-forth rocking motion. Early examples, advertised in American newspapers during the 18th century, had thick, solid-wood rockers shaped like half moons. Later examples had slender, curved rockers.

Collectors regard rocking horses, especially handmade examples, as folk art. Many such playthings sell for hundreds or thousands of dollars.

One important American manufacturer is Benjamin Crandall of Brooklyn, New York. Crandall produced rocking horses from the 1840s until the 1980s. Morton Converse of Rindge, New Hampshire, and Winchendon, Massachusetts, is another prominent company. Converse made rocking horses during the late 19th century.

Any marked rocking horse brings a high price. One marked with the name *Crandall* or *Converse* is especially valuable.

Some rocking horses are elaborately painted. Some have a leather harness. Others have manes and tails of real horsehair or cow hair. A few are completely covered with horsehide. Because hide-covered examples are usually in poor condition and look very realistic, most collectors prefer painted versions, which look more like toys.

SHOOFLIES

Hobbyhorses and rocking horses originated in Europe. The shoofly was invented in the United States. This toy is a rocker with a seat mounted between two flat sides. Some shooflies have sides shaped like horses. Others have sides shaped like cats, dogs, even swans. Some companies made rocking cradles with sides shaped like animals. Such cradles are rarer than shooflies.

VELOCIPEDES

Another popular 19th-century toy is the *velocipede*. The word *velocipede* is composed of two Latin words meaning *fast foot*. It usually refers to early bicycles. In toy collecting it refers to a type of child's tricycle.

The velocipede was a cart set on a pair of rear wheels and one front wheel. A horse's head was mounted above the front wheel.

Several American firms made velocipedes. E. W. Bushnell of Philadelphia made them during the 1840s and 1850s. A. Mecky Co. was another Philadelphia manufacturer. Its products are marked *Keystone*. Another maker was Christian & Son of New York City, which produced velocipedes from 1856 until the 1880s.

KIDDY CARS

Kiddy cars became popular during this century. Some consist of a seat and a steering post set on three or four wheels. Others are more elaborate. Some are shaped like animals or birds.

By 1920, the kiddy car had evolved into a "real" car. Many were wood, but most were sheet metal. These cars were pedal-operated and looked like full-sized autos, trucks or fire engines. They are among the most popular wheel toys. Rare examples from the 1920s cost thousands of dollars.

WAGONS AND SCOOTERS

Very few people collect wagons and scooters. Therefore, these playthings are easy to find and inexpensive.

Express wagons are sturdy vehicles with rail sides. Other wagons have sides shaped like dogs, cats, bears or other animals.

Some wagons have four wheels. Others have only two and are designed to be pushed like wheelbarrows.

Few scooters were made before 1930. Most scooters you will find were made in large factories. Some have two rear wheels, but most have a single wheel front and back. Look for scooters made during the 1930s. They have sleek, Art Deco fenders and are painted bright-red or blue.

COLLECTING HOBBYHORSES
AND WHEEL TOYS

Don't try to collect everything. You won't have room! Concentrate on one type of vehicle or one material.

Hobbyhorses and rocking horses are so popular that a few appear at almost every antique show and auction. They are expensive. You can sometimes find

This delicate late 19th-century elephant wheel toy has a bell that rings as you push or pull the toy. It costs $125 to $175.

bargains at house and barn sales. Most examples you will see at such sales were made after 1900.

Kiddy cars, velocipedes, wagons and scooters are easy to find. These toys are still stored in barns and attics. An ad in a local paper may bring excellent results. Describe what you want in detail, so readers will know exactly what you are looking for.

Like all painted-metal toys, wheel toys are most valuable when they have good, original paint. A repainted example or one with badly worn paint has lost 50% to 75% of its value.

BUYING AND SELLING
HOBBYHORSES AND WHEEL TOYS

● Because they are often large, these playthings are seldom collected in quantity. How many rocking horses, scooters or kiddy cars can you find room for? If you find a great old hobbyhorse tucked away in an attic, it may be very valuable. It may also be very difficult to sell.

● Look for wheelbarrows, sleds and wagons that are attractively painted and decorated. You can find these toys at flea markets and yard sales.

Child's *push-along* of wood and metal, made in the United States, 1950 to 1960. This foot-powered toy, 25 inches long, doesn't interest many collectors. It is worth $25 to $35. However, like construction toys of the 1930s, this toy will soon increase in value.

STEAM TOYS

Steam toys are steam-powered. Steam pressure causes them to move forward or perform specific actions. Most of these toys were made in the United States.

The steam toy is based on steam engines that powered 19th-century factory machinery and locomotives. Part of these toys' appeal results from this antiquated power source. Because they function and are so realistic, these toys bring the past to life. The engines are miniature versions of the real thing. The toys have heavy boilers in which water is heated to create steam. The steam drives the pistons. The boilers on most toys are heated, or *fired*, by kerosene or alcohol lamps. Some toys made in the 1930s and early 1940s use dry fuel. Most post-World War II examples use electricity.

TYPES OF STEAM TOYS

The three basic types of steam toys are *stationary engines, locomotives* and *traction engines.*

Stationary engines run machinery. Two basic types of stationary engines exist. One has a horizontal boiler, the other a vertical boiler.

Steam locomotives are trains. They are discussed in a later section of this book.

Traction engines pull things.

Many stationary engines were designed to run toy machines. Such machines include lathes, pumps and cutting tools used in early machine shops. Stationary engines can run other things, too. A complete steam-powered brewery was a popular novelty during Prohibition.

Because steam builds great pressure within the boiler, toy steam engines are made of strong materials. Steel and brass were often used. Even so, rusty pipes, faulty gauges and corrosion can cause boilers to explode. Never fire up a steam engine if you do not understand how it operates. Make sure the engine is in perfect working order. Children should never operate these toys without adult supervision.

AMERICAN MANUFACTURERS

Steam toys were made in Europe, especially in England and Germany. However, some interesting and well-made examples were produced in this country. Most American collectors prefer these.

Beggs and Buckman—Eugene Beggs of Patterson, New Jersey, and the Buckman Manufacturing Co. of New York City produced these toys. Both began operations in the 1870s and made steam toys until the turn of the century.

Weeden Manufacturing Co.—The most important American manufacturer was the Weeden Manufacturing

Lithographed tin-plate toy, made in Germany, 1900 to 1915. This clever toy can be operated either by a hand crank or by attaching a steam engine. One woodsman splits wood, the other saws. This example is 10 inches long and costs $75 to $160.

Steam toys, such as this accurate copy of an engine with a horizontal boiler, are not widely collected and are modestly priced at about $35 to $50.

Co. of New Bedford, Massachusetts. Weeden went into business in 1882 and started making steam toys two years later. The company's success resulted from product quality and cunning promotion. Weeden gave customers free subscriptions to boys' magazines such as *The Youth's Companion*. Few boys could resist the temptation to get both a toy and a magazine.

Weeden is still in business and is still making steam engines. In fact, one model was produced from 1884 until the late 1930s. You could form an attractive collection of Weeden steam engines and related toys.

ACCESSORIES

Various steam-engine accessories were usually driven by leather belts joining the accessory to the engine's drive shaft. These accessories included machines such as lathes and animated toys, and men chopping or sawing wood. Accessories were usually stamped steel or cast iron.

Some accessories were made by the same factories that made steam engines. Others were produced by tin-toy manufacturers. People unfamiliar with steam toys don't always recognize accessories. These playthings seem uninteresting when viewed by themselves, away from the toys they belong with.

COLLECTING STEAM TOYS

Few people collect steam toys, so these toys are usually inexpensive. The most costly steam toys are boats. They are very rare.

Steam engines and accessories can be found at antique and toy shows, auctions and yard sales. One interesting collection consists of several engines and their accompanying machine-shop accessories. Specialized collectors sometimes try to see how many different kinds of engines they can find.

These playthings are educational and amusing. They mirror the growth of our nation's industry, are technically interesting and provide hours of fun.

BUYING AND SELLING STEAM TOYS

- If you are mechanically inclined and enjoy playthings with moving parts, buy steam toys. They are much less expensive than most toys, partly because they are usually found in non-working condition. Repairs are easy. You can often buy a broken toy, fix it and sell it for 10 times what you paid.
- Remember that steam toys can be dangerous if used by people who don't know how to operate them. Never operate these toys if they are not in perfect working order. Always warn people to whom you sell steam toys that they must handle the toys with great care.

MILITARY MINIATURES

Children have played with toy soldiers for hundreds of years. As a collector, you will find thousands of different examples. Because these toys are fragile, most examples available today are less than 100 years old.

Toy soldiers are frequently referred to as *lead soldiers*. Don't let this confuse you. Few toy soldiers were pure lead. Toy soldiers are also called *military miniatures*. This is the term usually used by collectors.

Military miniatures have been made from many materials, including wood, metal, paper and cardboard, rubber, composition, and plastic. Collectors prefer metal figures.

WOOD SOLDIERS

The first military miniatures were wood. Their origins can be traced to the Middle Ages, but few examples exist that are more than 200 years old.

Wood soldiers were either hand-carved or cut out with a jigsaw. The hand-carved soldiers have round bodies and must be hand-painted. Those cut with a jigsaw can be painted or covered with lithographed decorations. These decorations can be applied directly to the toy or to paper glued to the toy.

TIN SOLDIERS

Tin soldiers have been made since the 1800s. They were cut or stamped from sheets of tin. They are hand-painted or lithographed, and are mounted on wood or metal bases. These soldiers are only popular with a few specialized collectors.

LEAD SOLDIERS

As early as the 13th century, manufacturers in the Magdeburg area of Germany were making lead soldiers. Cast in molds, these toys had uniforms shaped like those of various European armies. Most lead soldiers are miniature representations of real military units past or present. The accuracy of uniforms is very important to advanced collectors.

Several types of lead soldiers exist. The first is the *flat*. This is a two-dimensional figure with engraved decoration. Flats have been made for hundreds of years.

The second type is the *solid*. This is a three-dimensional metal figure. Solids are more realistic than flats, but they required so much metal that they were too costly for most buyers.

In 1893, Britains Ltd. of London invented a third type of lead soldier, the *hollow-cast*. This had a thin shell of lead alloy, making it inexpensive and light.

Cast pot-metal armored car and two tanks, 1960 to 1975. Left to right: Dinky Toys, England, $8 to $10; made in Japan, $12 to $18; Play Art, Hong Kong, $10 to $17. These examples are 3 inches to 6 inches long. Although not very old, these military vehicles are very collectible.

CAST-IRON SOLDIERS

Cast-iron soldiers are much harder to find than lead soldiers. Almost all cast-iron soldiers were made in the United States. Therefore, they are ideal for American collectors. The chief manufacturer was the Grey Iron Casting Co. of Mount Joy, Pennsylvania. This firm was founded in 1904.

Cast-iron soldiers are sturdy and attractive. They have one drawback. Iron is so difficult to cast that these soldiers come in only a few forms.

RUBBER SOLDIERS

During the 1930s and 1940s, a few American companies made rubber soldiers. The best-known manufacturer was the Auburn Rubber Co. of Auburn, Indiana. This firm, founded in 1913, made soldiers from 1935 until 1967.

Although they are fairly durable, rubber soldiers tend to lose their paint. Also, the bodies sag over time, especially in warm climates.

COMPOSITION SOLDIERS

Many types of composition soldiers exist. They are various mixtures of sawdust, glue and papier-mâché. The best-known type is Elastoline.

Introduced as a substitute for metal, Elastoline was less expensive and could often be molded into detailed figures. At least one American firm produced crude composition figures during the 1940s. Germany produced the greatest number. The increasing interest in composition soldiers results partly from the German influence. Many soldiers are modeled on the German Army troops of World War II. You may also find some representations of leading Nazi figures, including Adolf Hitler.

PAPER AND CARDBOARD SOLDIERS

Paper and cardboard soldiers are the least important category of military miniatures. Some are merely paper dolls shaped like soldiers. This group includes playthings produced by the famous English paper-doll manufacturer, Raphael Tuck. Others are thin cardboard covered with lithographed paper and mounted on wood bases.

These figures came in large sheets. The well-known American game manufacturer, McLoughlin Bros., produced enormous numbers of paper and cardboard soldiers. You can sometimes find complete McLoughlin sets in their original, decorated cardboard boxes. Such sets may be expensive. Incidentally, paper figures are worth far more in their original uncut sheets than they are as individual figures. If you find a sheet, don't cut it apart!

PLASTIC SOLDIERS

Since the early 1940s, most soldiers have been plastic. The earliest American manufacturer was Playwood Plastics of Brooklyn, New York. Some enthusiasts think this company's figures are collectible. Other collectors acquire lead-based plastic soldiers manufactured by Britains Ltd. of London. Most collectors show little interest in these playthings.

IMPORTANT MANUFACTURERS

Three-dimensional soldiers, primarily hollow-cast examples, are the most popular collectibles. If you intend to acquire military miniatures, you should know the famous manufacturers.

Britains Ltd. — At the top of the list is Britains Ltd. In fewer than 100 years, this company has produced thousands of authentically decorated soldiers and other figures. Such figures range from World War II military men to medieval knights and Roman warriors. These playthings usually have the Britains' stamp on the base. Britains Ltd. is especially famous for its boxed sets of soldiers representing Great Britain's most famous regiments.

Most American-made hollow-cast soldiers were sold individually rather than in sets. Many were sold in variety stores, and collectors call them *dime-store soldiers*.

These American-made figures are larger than their English and European counterparts, which are a standard 30mm (1.2 inches) tall. Some American-made soldiers have sheet-metal helmets that were made separately.

Set of flat cast-lead soldiers in 19th-century uniforms, made in France, 1910 to 1920. These figures cost $4 to $8 except for the cannoneer, which is $10 to $15. They are 2-1/2 inches to 3 inches high. These figures lack the quality of most hollow-cast 20th-century military miniatures.

Manoil and Barclay—The most important hollow-cast toy-soldier manufacturer was Manoil of Waverly, New York. This company began production in 1935 and closed during the 1950s. Another important manufacturer was Barclay Manufacturing Co. of Union City, New Jersey. It started making lead soldiers during the early 1930s and continued until after World War II.

Mignot of Paris—The best-known French manufacturer is Mignot of Paris, established about 1825. Mignot figures are often marked with a stamp on the base. Mignot made solid, flat and hollow-cast figures. These well-made soldiers are very popular.

George Heyde—Many German manufacturers produced solid, flat and a few hollow-cast figures. German miniatures are among the best-decorated. One well-known manufacturer was George Heyde of Dresden. This company went into business in 1870. It was destroyed during a World War II bombing raid.

Watch for toy-soldier accessories. Some match the scale of the figures. These include cannons, field guns, antiaircraft guns, tanks, trucks and jeeps. Britains Ltd. and various American, German and French firms produced these accessories. Incidentally, the Japanese did not make toy soldiers. However, they made some cast-metal versions of American tanks and field guns after World War II.

COLLECTING MILITARY MINIATURES

Early toy soldiers are usually available only at auctions or through specialized dealers. You can easily find recently made American dime-store metal and rubber soldiers. Most dime-store pieces sell for about $5. Rubber and composition figures cost $1 to $5. Figures by Britains Ltd. are also plentiful. Individual Britains foot soldiers in good condition bring $3 to $10 apiece. A rare complete set in its original box will often cost more than $1,000.

If you are starting a collection, concentrate on one type of military miniature. You might collect only lead soldiers or soldiers of one country. The field is so broad that even a collection of 1,000 figures would not be representative if it were not specialized.

American dime-store and early plastic soldiers are good investments. They are relatively inexpensive and easy to find. The origins of these soldiers are easy to trace because many catalogs still exist.

The delicate, hollow-cast Britains figures are also readily available.

Remember that condition is extremely important. Damage or loss of paint can lower the value of a piece 50% to 75%. Price differences between ordinary and rare soldiers are great. If you find what you feel is an unusual piece, check with an expert before you buy it.

Hollow-cast lead soldiers in World War II combat uniforms, Britains Ltd., London, 1950 to 1955. These figures are 2-1/2 inches high and cost $6 to $9 each. Britains developed the hollow-cast lead soldier and remains the most important manufacturer of military miniatures.

Scouts on Parade, lithographed paper on cardboard, McLoughlin Bros., New York City, 1920 to 1930. These toy soldiers cost $25 to $40 apiece and come in a brightly decorated cardboard box that is 12 inches by 21 inches. The soldiers are about 5 inches high. This set is similar to earlier cardboard and wooden soldiers.

BUYING AND SELLING MILITARY MINIATURES

• Look for complete sets. Many toy soldiers originally came in boxed sets of six, eight or 12 soldiers. A complete boxed set is much more valuable than the individual soldiers would be if sold separately.

• Never discard an empty box. You may be able to fill it with the appropriate soldiers.

• Collectors rate soldiers according to condition. The four ratings are fine, very good, good and average. *Fine* refers to a piece in unused condition. If you are going to build a collection, select only examples in the fine and very good range unless you find a rare example. With rare pieces, condition is less important.

TRAINS

Trains are gradually vanishing. They are being replaced by automobiles, trucks, planes and container ships.

Some of us seem to have forgotten how important trains once were. But one group still remembers. America's toy-train collectors are well aware of the glorious history of railroading in the United States. They have built this hobby into the largest area of toy collecting. They are so serious about their pastime that they call themselves *miniature railway enthusiasts*.

Many types of toy trains exist. You could collect wood, cast-iron or tin trains, trains that can be pushed or pulled, and trains with clockwork, steam or camphene engines. A few trains are friction-driven. Electric trains are the most popular.

AMERICAN TRAIN MANUFACTURERS

English and French manufacturers made very appealing toy trains. However, German and American manufacturers made most of the better sets.

George W. Brown & Co.—If you collect American trains, you will find a wide selection. The first tin clockwork trains were patented in 1856 by George W. Brown & Co. of Forestville, Connecticut. By the 1870s, the Ives Co. was producing hundreds of tin and cast-iron trains. These did not run on tracks. They were called *carpet runners*.

Secor and Bergmann—Cast-iron trains never became popular, probably because they were usually not motor-driven. Ives was one of several cast-iron train producers. Jerome Secor of Bridgeport, Connecticut, patented the first cast-iron train in the late 19th century. Another important name is Althof Bergmann & Co. of New York City.

Hubley and Carpenter—The Hubley and Francis Carpenter companies are also well-known manufacturers of trains and other cast-iron toys.

You may also find wood trains. As with most toy categories, wood examples are among the oldest. Early wood trains were hand-painted. Later examples were often covered with lithographed paper decorations. Wood trains and some cast-iron trains had friction motors.

Weeden Manufacturing Co.—About 1900, Weeden Manufacturing Co. started making steam-driven trains. These were very popular, especially with adults. They had two problems, however.

The first was a difficulty they shared with full-sized steam locomotives. As the steam condensed, it left puddles around the engine. This was such a nuisance that some English steam locomotive toys were called *puddlers* or *Birmingham dribblers*. Birmingham was the city in which many of these toys were made. The second problem was much more serious. Steam toys can explode if they are defective or handled improperly. This can result in serious injury. Don't operate a steam locomotive unless an expert has thoroughly checked it. Furthermore, you should understand exactly how to operate it.

ELECTRIC TRAINS

Electric trains were developed in the United States during the 1850s. Early electric trains were expensive and impractical. It was not until the 1880s that they were made in quantity. Two important American train manufacturers appeared during the early 1900s.

Lionel Manufacturing Corp.—The first was the Lionel Corp. of New York City, founded in 1901. Lionel was a pioneer in electric trains. It absorbed the bankrupt Ives Co. in 1931.

American Flyer Co.—The other well-known electric-train manufacturer was the American Flyer Co. of Chicago. American Flyer was in business from 1907 until it was taken over in 1938 by the A. C. Gilbert Co. of Chicago.

You can easily distinguish unmarked American trains from their European counterparts. American locomotives almost always have a cowcatcher on front.

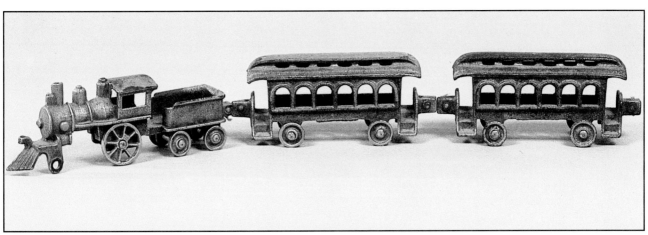

Cast-iron locomotive, tender and two coaches, Kilgore Manufacturing Co., Westerville, Ohio, 1925 to 1935. Total length of this train is 16 inches. It is worth $75 to $135. Most cast-iron trains were larger than this and brightly painted.

This is the grillwork that served to clear the track. With the exception of a few German trains exported to the United States, European locomotives don't have cowcatchers.

GERMAN TRAIN MANUFACTURERS

After the United States, Germany is the most important source of toy trains. The Germans were making wood carpet runners, or trackless trains, in the 1850s. They didn't make tin trains until the 1880s, but became a leader in the field during the early 20th century.

Märklin Bros.—German toy-train manufacturers made an important contribution to the world of miniature railway enthusiasts. In 1891, Märklin Bros. invented sectional, tin-plated tracks. This led to the development of complex track systems. Some extend through several rooms. With such long tracks, numerous accessories were needed. Stations, water towers, signal systems and baggage-handling facilities appeared. Today these accessories are in great demand. An elaborate tin or wood station by Ives or by a German manufacturer such as Märklin Bros. may cost several hundred dollars.

Bub and Bing—Leading German manufacturers include Karl Bub and Gebrüder Bing of Nüremberg. The latter once made a special silver-plated train for an Indian ruler. The wealthy gentleman used the train to carry wine bottles around his giant living-room table!

Although they also made windup and trackless trains, the Germans excelled in electrical and steam-powered trains. Advanced collectors prize these toys.

OTHER MANUFACTURERS

English and French manufacturers made toy trains. Well-known French manufacturers include Charles Rossignol and M. Radiquet of Paris. These firms specialized in well-made steam and pull-toy trains.

The major English producer, Frank Hornby, did not enter the field until 1920. The company still produces trains. English trains are well-made but are not available in sufficient quantities to interest most collectors.

COLLECTING TOY TRAINS

Toy-train collecting is very competitive. German and American trains from the late 19th and early 20th centuries are especially popular. Depending on condition and rarity, these trains can cost several thousand dollars. Complete sets are more expensive than individual cars and locomotives. Pieces in unusual sizes bring the highest prices. Such pieces include giant sets with cars 16 to 20 inches long, twice the usual length.

Don't be discouraged by high prices. Collectors with modest means can concentrate on several areas. Many windup and electric trains made from 1930 to 1960 are good buys. They often cost less than $100 per set. You may find good examples at antique shows, yard sales or secondhand shops. More popular trains are harder to find. You will have to attend auctions and contact specialized dealers.

Most collectors aren't interested in early wood trains. You can purchase them at reasonable prices. You may have trouble locating lithographed examples in good condition.

Trains probably constitute the most complex and sophisticated area of toy collecting. Be sure to read several books on the subject before you invest. You need to be knowledgeable. You can be sure most other collectors are!

Sheet-steel day coach for oversized railroad train, Lionel Manufacturing Corp., New York City, 1930 to 1940. Very large train components are popular with many collectors, and Lionel is a famous manufacturer. This example is 29 inches long and costs $300 to $375.

Electric locomotive and tender of sheet steel and cast iron, Märklin Bros., Göppingen, Germany, 1910 to 1920. The locomotive is 8-1/2 inches long. Märklin was one of the most important early European electric-train manufacturers. This train sells for $400 to $500.

BUYING AND SELLING TRAINS

• Buy trains made by well-known American or European manufacturers. Trains made by Ives, Lionel or Märklin will retain their value.

• Some enthusiasts collect only locomotives, but most people want entire trains. A complete set of matching cars will always be worth more than an engine and a few unmatched cars. A complete set in its original box will cost the most and will increase in value the fastest.

GAMES

European and American manufacturers have produced many different games during the past 100 years. These games fall into several categories. They comprise one of the most interesting and varied areas of toy collecting.

BOARD GAMES

Board games are probably the most popular type. These games come in boxes and are played on a board. Pieces, or *counters,* are advanced on the board toward a goal or finish line. The movement of the pieces is determined by casting dice, spinning a wheel or drawing cards.

Most board games are paper and cardboard. Early examples were engraved. After 1840, lithography was used. The games' bright colors and interesting graphics contribute to their popularity. Many collectors frame the board and the cover of the box.

Board games were made in England during the 18th century. They appeared in this country about 1850. Many are marked with the manufacturer's name and the date of issue. You can identify many manufacturers. Some are still in business.

AMERICAN MANUFACTURERS

You are probably familiar with the important names in American games. They include Parker Bros.; the Milton Bradley Co. of Springfield, Illinois; W. & S. B. Ives, McLoughlin Bros., and Selchow & Righter of New York City.

Parker Bros.—This firm was founded in 1883. In 1935, it introduced Monopoly, the most popular board game ever. Monopoly has been translated into many languages, and millions of copies have been sold.

W. & S. B. Ives—This company made the game with the longest name: Pope and Pagan or The Missionary Campaign or The Siege of the Stronghold of Satan by the Christian Army. This game was introduced in 1844, when society thought games should be morally and spiritually uplifting. Most board games made before 1850 taught religious principles and proper behavior. They were not meant for fun.

This approach changed during the second half of the 19th century. In the 1860s numerous war and patriotic games appeared. Manufacturers began producing practical or educational games. These games offered instruction in such diverse areas as business, household management and geography.

Selchow & Righter—Some games were also designed for family fun. One such game was Parcheesi, patented by Selchow & Righter, a firm founded in 1864.

McLoughlin Bros.—Numerous instructional and humorous games were made by this firm. It also produced paper and cardboard toys.

Wood Donald Duck bowling game, Pressman Toy Co., New York City, about 1950 to 1960. This game came in a 10- by 14-inch cardboard box and costs $7 to $12.

Action Baseball game of lithographed tin and wood, Pressman Toy Co., New York City, 1950 to 1960. Player holds back spring-loaded bat until marble "ball" is rolled forward. After being hit, ball rolls into holes in field. This game is 14 inches by 23 inches and costs $20 to $25.

TABLE GAMES

This category includes a remarkable number of indoor activities. Some of these games are miniature versions of larger, outdoor games. Horseshoes, bowling and tennis have table-game formats.

One of the most popular table games is the fishing set. McLoughlin Bros. made the early version, Magnetic Fish Pond, in 1891. Players use small poles with magnets attached to strings to "catch" metal fish.

Doctors' and nurses' sets are also popular. These games have educational value. They help children become familiar with and less afraid of medical personnel and hospitals.

Rare table games sell for several hundred dollars at auction. One example is a racehorse game. A player activates a system of weights that makes metal horses race around a track. Other examples are games in which metal balls fall from higher to lower elevations. The balls drop into cups marked with numbers. The person with the highest point total wins. Pinball machines were developed from these playthings.

CONSTRUCTION TOYS

Construction toys have been popular for more than a century. The earliest examples were building blocks or bricks made of wood or cut stone. The German firm D. Richter & Co. of Rudolstadt began producing these during the 1880s. Some sets had more than 300 pieces and were so large that a child could build a small house! A Richter set in its original box costs about $100.

The two best-known American construction toys are the Erector Set and Lincoln Logs.

The Erector Set was developed in 1913 by the A. C. Gilbert Co. of Chicago. Lincoln Logs were created in 1910 by J. L. Wright of Chicago.

Tenpin set, Ives, Blakelee & Co., Bridgeport, Conn., 1880 to 1900. Made of lithographed paper on wood, these figures were knocked over by a ball rolled at them. Each piece was worth a specific number of points. This set sells for $100 to $150. Figures are 4 inches to 5 inches high.

You may find metal building sets by Meccano. This company entered the toy business in 1901.

All these playthings were designed to enable children to erect buildings or make machinery and vehicles. This tradition continues today with the hard-plastic Lego sets, distributed by Lego Systems Inc. of Enfield, Connecticut. These are becoming collectors' items.

Table games and construction toys are not especially popular with collectors. There are two reasons for this:

1. These games are difficult to display.

2. These playthings often have many parts, making it difficult to determine whether a set is complete.

These problems also apply to less-popular construction toys, clay modeling and paint sets, and bead and needlework sets. If you want inexpensive games that are not widely collected, look at these fields.

COLLECTING GAMES

You can buy some games, especially early 19th-century examples and unusual animated types, from toy dealers. You can also find these games at auctions. Look

Horse-racing game, Jeu De Course, made in France, 1890 to 1910. This spring-driven game, worth $175 to $250, is one of the most popular racing toys. When the motor is released, the horses race around the track. Horses and posts are cast metal. The rest of the toy is wood and cloth. The game is 18 inches long and 12 inches wide. The figures are 2 inches high.

for other games at yard sales. You can sometimes buy McLoughlin and Milton Bradley games for a few dollars. Be sure to check the contents before you buy. An incomplete game is much less valuable than a complete example.

Antique dealers often have old games and construction toys. Dealers will usually sell these toys for $5 to $35 apiece. They will want more for rare or unusual early games. Remember that the condition of the box and board is very important. If these are faded, water-damaged or badly torn, the game has little resale value. There is no reason for you to "play" with real money!

Toyville Doctor Kit, wood, plastic, metal and cardboard, made in the United States, about 1945 to 1965. The kit came in a 5- by 10-inch cardboard box and costs $10 to $15. Doctors' and nurses' kits are seldom found intact or in unused condition.

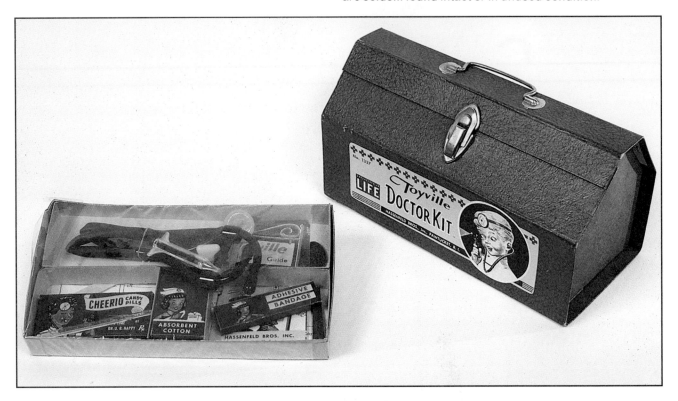

Mickey Mouse Club clay set, Pressman Toy Co., New York City, about 1960 to 1965. Clay sets are usually classified as construction toys. Because they do not interest many collectors, they are inexpensive. This set comes in an 8- by 13-inch cardboard box and sells for $5 to $9.

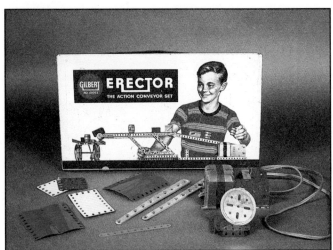

Sheet-metal Erector Set with electric motor, A.C. Gilbert Co., Chicago, about 1935 to 1950. When buying construction toys, make sure all original parts are present. This set comes in a metal box that is 11 inches by 20 inches. It is worth $20 to $35.

EDUCATIONAL TOYS

Most toys are designed to appeal to children. Some toys are also designed to introduce children to the adult world. You can probably remember the educational toys you had as a child. As an adult you can enjoy another aspect of these toys: collecting them.

SEWING MACHINES

One important educational plaything is the toy sewing machine. Full-sized sewing machines were first manufactured in the 1860s. Toy versions appeared about 1880. They are still being made.

The earliest toy sewing machines worked the same way as the real thing. By the 1930s, these tiny machines had been simplified and were more like toys.

Look for choice examples. Singer toys are especially interesting. They were just like the company's real sewing machines. F.W. Muller of Berlin also made a popular version of this toy. Machines shaped like animals, clowns, girls and other figures are also valuable.

HOUSEHOLD TOYS

Many other household items have toy versions. Miniature stoves, washing machines, pumps, sinks and

Wood blocks decorated with lithographed paper, made in the United States, 1890 to 1910. The set costs $40 to $70. Each block is 2-1/2 inches square. Some blocks display the alphabet, others make a picture or puzzle. The more attractive the lithography, the more desirable the blocks. Sets with missing pieces have little value.

refrigerators provide children with a great deal of fun.

Stoves—Toy stoves were first made in the mid-19th century. Some toy stoves are very simple. Others are very realistic. Some are so realistic that you can cook on them! These toy stoves burn coal or wood, but a few run on kerosene, cooking gas or electricity. Be careful when operating such playthings.

Washing Machines—These toys are amusing. You could put together an entertaining collection of nothing more than toy washboards. You can find wood, tin, glass and pottery examples.

The first toy washing machines, manufactured in the late 19th century, were simply wringers attached to tubs. By the 1930s, toy washing machines had been modernized. Some even had clear-glass sides, allowing you to watch the wash go around. Some were powered by electricity.

Pumps—Until the 20th century, most people used pumps to draw water. Toy pumps were first manufactured in the mid-19th century. Many still exist. Most are tin. Some have a single pump. Others have two. Some can be hooked up to a water source. Others have their own reservoirs.

Sinks and Refrigerators—These playthings were introduced during the 1920s. The best actually function. The plumbing for toy sinks is very simple. A small bottle of water is attached to the outside or back of the toy. Water flows from the bottle through the faucets.

Some toy refrigerators function, too. They have a place for a piece of ice. The ice keeps the refrigerator cold.

SHOP AND OFFICE TOYS

Not all educational toys were related to the home. As America developed in the mid-19th century, many people left their homes to seek work in business and industry. Toys relating to the shop and the office soon appeared. This is natural. Most children seek to imitate their parents. Miniature versions of objects that represent drudgery to adults can bring joy to the young.

Cash Registers—The first such toys included miniature cash registers. Some, like the popular Tom Thumb, were made of sheet steel decorated with paint and decals. The Tom Thumb originally sold for a few cents. Late 19th-century brass, wood and marble cash registers are rarer and more valuable. They sometimes cost hundreds of dollars.

Typewriters—These have been around since the 1870s. Mark Twain was one of the first authors to use a typewriter. He wrote *The Adventures of Tom Sawyer* on one of the earliest models.

Toy typewriters made before 1900 are rare. Most of these miniature machines were made between 1920 and 1950. Except for very old or ornate examples, these playthings usually aren't expensive. Many different types are available.

COLLECTING EDUCATIONAL TOYS

Educational toys are not especially popular, so you can buy them at reasonable prices. Look for them at antique stores, toy shops, flea markets and secondhand stores. Try advertising for these playthings. You might get excellent buys. Most collectors concentrate on one

The Unique Dependable toy typewriter of lithographed tin, Unique Art Manufacturing Co., Newark, N.J., 1950 to 1960. Toy typewriters are plentiful and underpriced. This example is 12 inches long and costs $20 to $50.

Toy sewing machine of sheet steel, Gateway Co., Chicago, 1930 to 1945. This toy is 7 inches high and costs $50 to $80. You can build a large collection of different sewing machines.

Toy cash register of sheet steel and glass, Western Stamping Co., Detroit, 1945 to 1960. Larger, more realistic registers bring higher prices. This toy, called the *Tom Thumb,* functioned like a real machine. It is 7-1/2 inches high and sells for $25 to $75.

type of educational toy, such as sewing machines.

Because this field has not been widely explored by collectors, you can be a pioneer. Track down the types that appeal to you and share what you learn with other collectors.

Toy double water pump of lithographed tin plate, made in Germany, 1920 to 1930. This piece is 13 inches long and costs $80 to $120. Water from a concealed reservoir can be released through the pumps.

PLASTIC TOYS

Toy collecting is not the same as antique collecting. Most toys are not old enough to be considered antiques. Many collectible toys were made after 1900.

This is a good thing. It means you don't have to be concerned about the age of the toys you collect. You can collect what you like. You can even choose contemporary playthings, such as plastic toys.

CONTEMPORARY COLLECTIBLES

Plastics are organic compounds, such as resins and cellulose. These compounds are mixed, reduced to a liquid, then cast in molds. The first plastic was celluloid. Manufacturers used it for playthings in the early 20th century.

Toy makers started using plastics extensively after World War II began. Cast iron and lighter metals, such as white metal and tin, were requisitioned for military use. Manufacturers then turned to plastics. They often cast plastics in the same molds they had used for metals.

Buyers didn't like the new material at first. But manufacturers did. It was cheaper and easier to handle than metal, and it lent itself to mass production. When the war ended, most toy makers continued to use plastics. Today, most toys are at least partly plastic.

COLLECTING PLASTIC TOYS

If you want to explore a new area of toy collecting, plastics may be the field you're looking for. Manufacturers have produced thousands of plastic toys since 1940. These include such popular toys as the *Star Wars* figures and the Smurfs. You may wonder why you should consider collecting toys made so recently. During the past 50 years, collectors have learned that toys that are popular when new are popular when old. This is especially true of toys based on movie, television or cartoon characters. *Star Wars* toys and Smurfs are good investments.

Don't let the large number of today's plastic toys fool you. Toys disappear. Toys that were popular in 1950 had vanished by 1980. Barbie dolls are an excellent example. Tens of thousands of little girls had one during the 1970s. Today, rarer examples cost $300.

You have a wide choice of plastic toys. The oldest examples date from the early 1900s and are usually thin, fragile celluloid. This crude plastic isn't popular with most collectors because the toys aren't attractive.

Moreover, many celluloid toys made between World War I and World War II were produced in Japan. Many of these toys were poor quality. Don't confuse these toys with the fine-quality plastic toys produced in Japan during the 1960s and 1970s.

Solid molded-plastic circus animals and cages, Fisher-Price Ltd., East Aurora, N.Y., 1950 to 1980. These toys are 3 inches to 3-1/2 inches high. Fisher-Price Ltd. is a leading producer of high-quality plastic toys. Readily available now, they will soon become hard-to-find collectibles. Today they are worth $3 to $5 each.

American and European manufacturers produced few plastic toys before 1940. Attractive examples from this period are valuable. American companies made many types of plastic toys after World War II. Quality differs greatly. The best include the fine, hard-plastic figures made by firms such as Creative Playthings. Cars and ships from the 1950s and 1960s are plentiful. These inexpensive toys interest very few collectors.

If you plan to collect plastic toys, pay special attention to quality. If a toy looks as if it will fall apart, don't buy it.

WHAT TO LOOK FOR

Because they are easy to find and inexpensive, plastic toys offer the collector unusual opportunities. You can collect complete sets, or *runs,* from one manufacturer.

If a company made six types of plastic airplanes, buy all six. Each plane is worth more when it's part of a group.

Look for toys in their original boxes. Sometimes you can also find the literature that was originally enclosed with the toy. These items increase the value of any plaything.

You can buy collectible plastic toys at yard sales, church bazaars, flea markets and secondhand stores. You probably won't find any at antique shows or through toy dealers.

Collect these toys as quickly as possible. Rare examples are still relatively easy to find, but as collectors' interest increases, valuable toys will become difficult to acquire.

Many plastic toys cost between $1 and $5. However, some examples cost several hundred dollars. One plastic, battery-powered robot made in Japan recently sold for $1,000.

Plastic toys are a wonderful field for beginning collectors and those with limited funds. These playthings are fun and easy to locate. Buy only complete, undamaged examples.

BUYING AND SELLING PLASTIC TOYS

- Very few people collect plastic playthings made after the early 1940s. These toys are often sold for a few pennies at yard sales. If you know what to look for, you can assemble a wonderful collection.
- Toys modeled after well-known characters are always good buys. Their value will probably increase more rapidly than that of anonymous toys. Superheroes and comic-strip characters are especially popular.
- When storing plastic toys, keep them in a cool, dry, dark place. Plastics, especially older types, sometimes deteriorate if exposed to sunlight or dampness.

Smurfs are among the most popular collectibles around today. Some of the earliest models like the ones above are already drawing high prices. Those pictured here are valued at $20 to $30 each.

MISCELLANEOUS TOYS

Some toys fit into small, specialized categories not explored in detail in this book. These include very new toys and playthings produced continuously for many years. Some of these categories include very few examples, but all have enthusiastic collectors.

AUTOMATONS

Automatons, or *automata,* as they are sometimes called, are clockwork-driven figures that perform complex movements. Most automatons have the same basic spring-wound motor used in tin clockwork toys. However, automatons have more intricate structures than other clockwork toys. Automatons usually have doll-like bodies with composition or porcelain heads, legs and arms. Most are dressed in doll clothing made of cloth.

These toys were developed during the 16th century. Some of the finest examples were made during the 18th century by French and Swiss manufacturers. These expensive playthings were usually designed for adults' amusement. Automatons in good working condition cost several hundred dollars each. Few examples or large collections exist outside museums.

NODDING-HEAD TOYS

Nodding-head toys are easier to find than automatons. They are wood, composition or papier-mâché human and animal figures. The figures' heads and bodies are joined by springs or a series of wires and weights. When the toys are touched, the heads move up and down.

Nodding-head toys are also called *nodders.* They are usually unmarked. American and European manufacturers produced numerous examples. The most valuable include toys shaped like comic-strip characters such as Donald Duck and Mickey Mouse. Rare examples in good condition may cost $100. Most nodding-head toys cost much less.

These toys are usually small. You could acquire two- or three-dozen different figures.

BATTERY-POWERED TOYS

This category is large. Some battery-powered toys were made during the 1930s, but most were produced after World War II. Early examples are tin. Contemporary examples are pot metal, plastic or a combination of materials.

Look for early remote-controlled toys. These toys are operated by a small hand-held unit. You can make

Automaton, or mechanical doll, made in France or Germany, 1900 to 1915. Really "toys" for adults, automatons are remarkably complex and can do fascinating things. This example, 13 inches high, is worth $300 to $450. Its head, hands and feet are porcelain. Its body is cloth.

Composition-and-cloth marionettes, made in the United States, 1950 to 1960.
Left: Pinocchio, 14 inches high, $75 to $110. Right: Howdy Doody, 17-1/2
inches high, $100 to $150. Marionettes and puppets based on radio, television
or comic-strip characters are especially valuable.

Battery-operated mechanical poodle, made in Japan, 1950 to 1960. This cloth-and-artificial-fur dog is typical of many mechanical animals made in Japan from 1950 to 1970. All are attracting collectors' attention. This toy is 9 inches high and costs $25 to $35.

Lithographed-tin and molded-plastic robots, made in Japan, 1955 to 1970. Left to right: Roto Robot, 8-1/2 inches high, $25 to $30; silver robot, 9-1/2 inches high, $30 to $45; laser robot, 7 inches high, $100 to $140; unmarked robot, 5 inches high, $20 to $25. Robots are rapidly increasing in value. Prices vary depending on rarity and size.

them move in any direction without touching them. Remote-controlled toys were first made in the 1950s. Collectors' interest in them is increasing.

ROBOTS AND SPACE TOYS

A few Buck Rogers-type rocket ships and robots appeared during the 1930s. Space toys arrived in quantity in the 1950s. Some are battery-operated, some are clockwork-driven. They come in various materials and fanciful shapes.

Space-Age toys have captured many collectors' imaginations. The most sought-after examples include those made in Japan from 1950 until the late 1970s. Rare examples from this period cost several hundred dollars. Space toys by Louis Marx and other American manufacturers are also popular and less expensive.

OPTICAL TOYS

This category includes such playthings as magic lanterns, peep shows and kaleidoscopes. These toys project images or enable you to view objects in an unusual way. Magic lanterns are the predecessors of movie projectors.

Many museums have extensive collections of optical toys. Few private collectors are interested in these toys, for two reasons:

1. With the exception of the magic lantern, optical toys are usually hard to find. Most were made before 1900. As the motion-picture projector and the camera became popular, these early devices disappeared.

2. Because these toys had many fragile parts, few examples are intact.

COLLECTING MISCELLANEOUS TOYS

Battery-operated toys, robots and space toys are easy to find. Look in secondhand stores and relatives' attics. Go to auctions and yard sales. You can often find toys from the 1950s, 1960s and 1970s.

You can buy these toys from dealers, but you will probably have more fun and spend less money if you track them down yourself.

You may have to buy nodding-head toys from dealers. These toys are difficult to find.

Optical toys and automatons are also rare. Check with specialized antique or toy dealers. Also try advertising in collectors' publications.

Specialized dealers and collectors often get to know one another. They frequently buy and trade among themselves. You will find this interesting and fun. After all, toys were meant to be shared.

Painted tin and sheet-metal magic lantern, Ernst Plank Co., Nüremberg, Germany, 1910 to 1920. Magic lanterns were the forerunners of slide projectors. This example is 7 inches high and sells for $70 to $95.

Building a Collection

After you decide what to collect, the fun and excitement begin. Collecting toys is like searching for lost treasure. The toys you want are out there somewhere. Looking for them can be an adventure.

WHERE TO LOOK

Starting a collection is easy. You can choose from many different toy categories. Each includes numerous examples. You will probably have no difficulty finding your first purchases. As you expand your collection, you may have problems finding what you want. That makes the search more exciting. Your new acquisitions will be rare playthings. You will begin assembling an unusual collection.

You may find a few toys in dumps, but such playthings are usually badly damaged or have lost their paint.

Attics, sheds and cellars are better places to look. Toys may have been put away in these places and then forgotten.

Old barns and outbuildings sometimes have interesting toys. In days gone by, children loved to play in such "secret" places, and sometimes they left playthings behind. If you wish to explore old homes and barns, get the owners' permission first. Otherwise, you will be trespassing.

Always be careful when searching old buildings. Many are in poor condition. Watch for rotten floorboards, holes in the floor, and broken glass or other sharp objects. Making a great find isn't worth injuring yourself.

Check local antique shops and shows. Most antique dealers have a few toys. Although most of these playthings are ordinary, a few could be rare. Many antique dealers don't recognize unusual playthings, so you may get an unusual toy at a very low price.

BUYING FROM DEALERS AND COLLECTORS

You will probably find that you will have to purchase most of the toys you want from dealers or collectors.

Specialized dealers have good selections. Don't expect bargains. Dealers know exactly how much the toys they have are worth. Get acquainted with specialized dealers in your area. Honest, knowledgeable dealers will provide you with quality toys in good condition. They can also give you important information about your hobby. After establishing a relationship with several dealers, you will find that your search for toys will be easier. The dealers will help you find the special toys you want.

BUYING AT AUCTIONS

You can also find old playthings at auctions. Toys are included in most house or estate auctions. You may be the only toy collector present. With no other collectors or dealers to compete with, you may find some real bargains.

Buying toys at auctions can be tricky. The auctioneer may not know much about toys or may misrepresent their condition. *Always* attend the pre-sale viewing and examine the toys carefully.

Auctions can be exciting, but don't get carried away. Pay no more at an auction than you would at a shop or show.

Several large toy auctions are held in the United States each year. Try to attend at least one. These auctions will provide a wider selection than you could find elsewhere. You will also have the opportunity to meet dealers and collectors from all over the country. Prices for the best pieces are usually high, but prices for ordinary examples are reasonable.

As you become a more advanced collector, you will have more difficulty finding the toys you want. Try advertising in your local newspapers. It is inexpensive and may lead to some excellent bargains. Also advertise in toy collectors' magazines.

CHOOSING A CATEGORY

Many people don't have a category before beginning their collections. They acquire a few examples of

A fascinating collection of 19th- and 20th-century toys in wood, tin, cast-iron and pot metal. Most collectors would specialize in one of these areas rather than collecting them all.

several kinds of toys. Eventually they realize how large and expensive a general collection can be, and begin thinking about specializing. Most collectors focus on one or two categories. The problem is how to choose an appropriate category. You should follow these rules:

1. Collect toys that you like. No matter how numerous and inexpensive one type of toy may be, don't collect it if you don't like it. Collecting should be fun, not work. Many types of toys are available, so you should have little difficulty finding one that pleases you.

2. Buy selectively. If you have $30 you might be inclined to buy 15 pieces at $2 each instead of 3 pieces at $10 each. Knowledgeable collectors and dealers know that this would be a mistake. Buying more expensive pieces is almost always wiser. Such toys will usually increase in value more quickly than less-expensive playthings. In addition, more costly pieces are usually

If you want to specialize as a collector, you might focus on an interesting area such as the cast-iron mechanical banks shown here.

Children often hide toys in out-of-the-way places, then forget about them. Always check under stairs, in old cupboards and on high shelves. You never know what you might find.

Collectors specializing in mechanical toys would be interested in this Ferris wheel.
So would collectors specializing in Mickey Mouse memorabilia.

harder to find, so you should buy them when you see them.

BUYING AND SELLING TOYS

Toy collecting is popular with many specialized dealers and collectors. Because it is such a large, well-organized field, toy collecting has become like a business. Most toy prices are fairly stable. Price guides, such as the one in this book, are very useful. Most collectible toys were made in factories in large quantities. Prices are well-established for most playthings. However, prices for rare toys may vary greatly.

Most toy collectors eventually sell some of their toys. If you plan to buy or sell toys, try to determine average prices. Examine the price guides. Attend auctions. Talk to dealers.

Wholesale and retail prices are different. If you sell a toy to another collector, you can charge a retail price. That is, you can charge what a dealer would charge. If you are selling the same type of toy to a dealer, you must charge a wholesale price. This is 30% to 50% lower than a retail price. Dealers pay wholesale prices because they must cover their overhead and make a profit when they resell a toy.

Most antique shops have at least a few toys to sell. A little hunting will often yield a valuable toy.

DISPLAYING YOUR COLLECTION

The sizes of your toys and the number you have will determine how you display them. Few collectors have enough room to display more than six wheel toys, which are very large. However, collectors can display entire regiments of toy soldiers on one small shelf.

Toys should be displayed in a manner that protects them and brings out their best qualities. Smaller toys, such as tin windup toys, lead soldiers and cast-iron vehicles, look very attractive on shelves. You may want to put glass in front of the shelves. If the toys wobble, attach them to the shelves. You can use an adhesive, such as photographers' gum or two-sided tape. Larger toys, such as automatons and clockwork carousels, can be mounted on pedestals or blocks. You can display them as you would a piece of sculpture.

Never expose toys to direct sunlight, heat or cold. Sunlight causes paint to fade. Heat and cold cause wood figures to crack or separate. Dampness is also harmful. It causes glued joints to rot and deteriorate. A good rule is to care for your finest toys as you would a valuable painting or carving.

You can display the playing surfaces and box covers of board games as you would paintings. You can mount them on a wall, place them under glass or put them under the glass top of a coffee table.

Some toys, such as magic lanterns and kaleidoscopes, look best when they are in operation. Display these toys where your family and friends can use them.

A shelf unit such as this one is easy to build and lets people see your collection from all sides.

Here is a nice way to display a collection of board games.

STORING YOUR TOYS

You probably won't be able to display all your toys all the time. Some will have to be stored. You may also have to move your collection someday. Storing and moving toys is not difficult.

Small toys should be stored in wood or strong cardboard boxes. The inside dividers of boxes can be used to keep individual toys separated. Wrap toys in a soft material. Disposable diapers work well. Various kinds of plastic wrapping materials are also available.

Handle toys carefully. Painted tin toys and paper toys with lithographed paper decorations are especially delicate. Don't expose them to sudden shocks or to pressure that could make their decorations flake off.

Dampness is especially damaging to paper, wood and rubber toys. Never store them in a humid place, such as a cellar.

If rubber or plastic toys are stored too long in one position, some parts may flatten. Change the positions of these toys every six months.

Make sure no mice are in your house. Rodents like to eat the glue used on old toys. These pests will gnaw through boxes to get at an especially tasty plaything.

CLEANING AND REPAIRING TOYS

A little cleaning is usually enough. Dip a soft cloth in warm water with a mild detergent. Wring out excess water, then gently rub the cloth over the toy. This will remove accumulated dirt.

Don't use brushes, especially wire brushes. They can damage or remove painted decorations. Most glues used in toy making are water-soluble, so don't immerse a plaything in water. Put a thin coat of light oil on cast-iron or tin toys after cleaning them. This will retard rust. Some collectors apply linseed oil to old wood toys to restore the natural wood oils. Other collectors prefer not to do this because it darkens the surface.

Most experienced collectors don't try to restore or

Pack toys carefully if you have to store or move them. Use soft materials, such as disposable diapers or Styrofoam packing material.

Soap and water are often enough to clean an old toy. But if you need something stronger, try a diluted ammonia solution. Don't use steel wool or other abrasive. It might scratch the finish.

repair toys. Restoration and repair are complex matters. To do them properly, you *must* know what the toy looked like originally. You must also know about metal work, soldering and painting. Most collectors agree that bad restoration work lowers the value of a toy. Consult a professional restorer or leave the piece as is. If you want to have a toy restored, get a written estimate. You may decide it is too expensive.

The easiest way to minimize problems is to buy toys only in good condition.

RESEARCHING YOUR TOYS

Most collectors like to learn about their acquisitions. They want to know where, when and by whom their toys were made. Collectors have no problem learning about toys produced after 1880. Most of these have manufacturers' marks. Before 1880, many toys were sold by middlemen who didn't want shopkeepers to know who had manufactured the playthings. These

The damaged decoration on this toy decreases its value. Remember that any damaged toy will be difficult to resell.

This collector is pointing to the stamped trademark on a tin toy. Always check for such marks. A toy with a known maker is usually worth more than an unidentified plaything.

dealers were afraid that if the storekeepers learned the manufacturers' names, they would buy directly from the companies.

Board games are always marked. Many 20th-century tin toys are marked, too.

If a toy has a manufacturer's mark, it is easy to learn its history. Begin by referring to this book or to one of the others listed in the bibliography. Some books deal with one specific kind of toy, such as lead soldiers, trains or tin toys. Some give more general information. Other books discuss specific toy-making companies, such as Steiff.

Don't give up if books don't contain any information about your toy. You may be able to learn about it other ways. If you know which company made the toy, you can probably find out where the firm was located.

You can then write to the historical societies in that area. Such organizations can provide information about the manufacturer.

If the city you live in has a large library, your job will be easier. Most libraries have reference sections. Using the materials there, you can track down the history of your toy. Before 1930, most communities had business directories that listed the firms operating in the area. After 1930, telephone directories performed the same function. By looking through these directories, you should be able to find the company that made your toy. You might even locate one of the company's catalogs and find a picture of your toy.

This research is like detective work. When you finish your sleuthing, you may know more about your toy than anyone in the world.

Trains comprise one major area of toy collecting.
You could specialize in windup trains or tin trains.
This example could go in either collection.

ORGANIZING YOUR COLLECTION

It is important to keep track of your toys. You can do this by creating a record of your acquisitions. Such a record can be very helpful if you have to file insurance claims. You can also use it to plan future acquisitions.

The easiest way to make a record is to assign each toy a number, a letter or a combination of the two. Put this code on the bottom of the toy. If you collect several different types of toys, use a different code for each type. Enter the name and code number of each toy in a record book. Then list other useful information, including the seller's name, the price, and the place and date of purchase. You can also list the toy's history, including the manufacturer's name and location.

As your collection expands, you may forget the history of each toy if you don't write it down. By looking at the code number on a toy and then referring to your record book, you will instantly have all the facts. If you sell a toy, write the price and date in your book. Everything will then be accounted for.

PHOTOGRAPHING TOYS

Photographs are very useful. Many insurance companies require them. If you decide to insure your collection, you will also need an appraisal. This is an estimate of each toy's value. A dealer, an auctioneer or any other qualified person can make an appraisal. This person can use all the information you have acquired about your toys. The more information you have, the easier it will be to get an adequate insurance settlement if your toys are damaged, lost or stolen.

Most toys are not difficult to photograph. You will need a backdrop. A piece of cardboard, plywood or white cloth works well. Put the backdrop behind the toy. Light the area well, then take the picture. Use a 35mm camera and color film if you can.

Photograph one toy at a time. Put a copy of the slide or photograph in your record book. Mark each photograph with the toy's code number.

Researching and photographing your toys is worthwhile for many reasons. Even if you never lose or sell a single toy, the information and photographs are important. You will learn a great deal about the toys and the time in which they were made.

TOY COLLECTOR'S RECORD BOOK

CODE # _____

TYPE OF TOY _____

DATE OF PURCHASE _____

CONDITION _____

PURCHASE PRICE _____

ASSESSED VALUE _____

SOURCE OF ACQUISITION _____

_____

MANUFACTURER (IF KNOWN) _____

DESCRIPTION

    SIZE _____

    COLOR _____

    SHAPE _____

    LABEL _____

    MATERIALS USED _____

    DISTINGUISHING MARKS _____

_____

RESEARCH

    PUBLICATIONS OR EXPERTS CONSULTED _____

_____

_____

    RESULTS OF RESEARCH _____

_____

_____

NOTES _____

_____

_____

Consider copying this page many times to create a
record book for your toy collection.

Price Guide

Toys can bring as much joy to adults who collect them as they brought to the children who played with them. Like most toy collectors, you probably love your collection for its beauty and its nostalgic appeal. Like most collectors, you are probably also concerned with the value of your toys. You certainly don't want to pay more for a toy than it is worth. Likewise, you don't want to sell one of your toys too cheaply. This price guide will help you determine the value of the pieces you own or want.

ABOUT DEALERS

The prices given here are guides to value—not guarantees. The prices of toys, like other collectibles or antiques, cannot be firmly established. Old toys are hard to acquire. Because of this, there is no clear and simple way to determine the value of collectible toys. If a dealer sells you a Dogpatch Band, it may be months or years before he finds another. What he pays for the next piece will differ from what he paid for the first. The price he charges his next customer will also be different. As a rule, the seller determines selling price based on his purchase price.

This is only a general rule, however. A dealer's price also includes overhead and a profit margin—usually 15% to 25%. But original cost is the key factor, and costs vary. For this reason, two dealers may offer you the same item at different prices. Prices may vary by 15% to 25%.

ABOUT THIS PRICE GUIDE

This price guide is designed to compensate for such differences. Prices are given as a range, such as $40 to $55.

This book can't list prices for all available collectible toys. Indeed, no book could. We have selected and priced key toys from each category. These prices will give you an idea of the costs of comparable toys.

Condition—Prices given here are for toys in good, average condition. This means that they show normal wear, but are undamaged and have no missing parts. Damage, faded or chipped paint, and similar factors decrease a toy's price by as much as 25% to 75%.

Never pay a premium price for a damaged toy unless it is truly rare. Buy a damaged toy only if you are certain that you will never be able to buy a similar one.

Toys that have been altered from their original state are less valuable than unaltered toys. Alteration may include repainting, restoring and resoldering. Although many toys are repainted and restored these days, most collectors seek only unretouched pieces. Examine a toy closely to be sure that it has not been altered. If it has, pay less for it.

Supply and Demand—Prices, of course, are based on supply and demand. Even a rare toy will be inexpensive if no one wants it. The more people that want it, the higher a toy's price. This is particularly true of toys sought by different types of collectors. For example, Mickey Mouse toys are collected by toy collectors and collectors of Disney memorabilia. Such toys may also interest collectors of movie memorabilia. This type of competition stimulates high prices.

Prices are easier to establish for some toys than others. Mass-produced, factory-made playthings are widely available. Such toys are bought and sold so frequently that prices have been established. However, one-of-a-kind, hand-crafted toys are difficult to price. You can't easily compare these toys to others.

ABOUT AUCTIONS

Auction often provide a fairly good guide to toy prices. Toys are sold at specialized auctions and in general antiques auctions, too. However, competition among bidders can push auction prices higher than most dealer prices. Because of this, dealer prices are usually the best indication of market value.

Painted-wood pecking chicken toy, probably made in Russia, 1940 to 1960.
Toys like this have been made for centuries. This example is 4 inches high and
costs $7 to $12.

Set of painted dolls, made in Russia, 1950 to 1960. These wood toys, 2 inches
to 3-1/2 inches high, fit inside one another. They were a popular import and
cost $5 to $9.

Stable of lithographed cardboard, paper and wood, with painted-wood horse and cart, probably made by R. Bliss Manufacturing Co., Pawtucket, R.I., 1910 to 1920. Bliss made many houses, barns and stables. They are all popular with collectors. This example, 8 inches long, costs $75 to $150.

These stuffed animals are good examples of the smaller soft toys produced by Steiff. Left: Donkey, $50 to $65. Right: Seal, $60 to $80.

Four painted tin-plate boats, 1920 to 1935. Left to right: Speedboat, Matheis Hess, Nüremberg, Germany, 11 inches long, $90 to $130; ocean liner, Wolverine Co., Pittsburgh, 14-1/2 inches long, $45 to $60; clockwork-powered speedboat, Ives Co., Bridgeport, Conn., 9 inches long, $200 to $250; ocean liner, made in Germany, 8 inches long, $40 to $50.

Soft toys of plush and fur fabric, Steiff, Giengen an der Brenz, Germany, 1930 to 1950. Left to right: Turkey, 6 inches high; wheel rabbit, 3-1/2 inches high; rabbit, 8 inches high; deer, 5 inches high. These pieces cost $50 to $90 each. Steiff soft toys are the most popular and expensive.

Lithographed tin-plate Merrymakers clockwork musical toy, Louis Marx & Co., New York City, 1930 to 1935. This is one of the most popular Marx toys. It is the forerunner of the popular Howdy Doodie Band. This toy is 12 inches long and costs $350 to $550.

Tin-plate buses with lithographed decoration, made in Japan, 1945 to 1960. Left to right: Double decker, 8 inches long; double decker, 7 inches long; avenue bus, 9 inches long; Greyhound, 8-1/2 inches long. Tin toys made in Japan after World War II are good investments. These pieces cost $15 to $25 each.

Lithographed tin-plate clockwork toys, 1930 to 1940. Left to right: Charlie McCarthy, Louis Marx & Co., New York City, $75 to $100; Popeye the Sailor, Julius Chein Manufacturing Co., Harrison, N.J., $125 to $175; Donald Duck, made by an unknown American manufacturer, $50 to $75; Mortimer Snerd, Louis Marx & Co., $150 to $250. These figures are 6 inches to 9 inches high.

Painted and lithographed tin-plate musical toys, made in the United States. Left to right: Toy bugle, 6-1/2 inches high, $5 to $8; sparkle toy, 10 inches high, $40 to $65; top, 5-1/2 inches in diameter, $4 to $8; rolling toy, 23 inches long, $7 to $12. The sparkle toy was made from 1918 to 1922. The others were made from 1930 to 1940.

Painted tin-plate toy horns, made in the United States, 1890 to 1910. Children used these horns during Fourth of July, New Year's and other celebrations. They are attractive and inexpensive collectors' items. These examples are 6 inches to 12 inches high and cost $5 to $12 each.

Cast-iron fire-department hose reel, Kenton Hardware Co., Kenton, Ohio, 1900 to 1910. This firefighting toy is 19-1/2 inches long and sells for $200 to $300.

Cast-iron construction toys, Kenton Hardware Co., Kenton, Ohio, 1920 to 1930. Left: Road roller, 8-1/2 inches long. Right: Cement mixer, 6-1/2 inches long. Inexpensive and attractive, toy construction vehicles such as these are popular with collectors. These playthings sell for $60 to $90 each.

Cast-iron parcel-post deliveryman with motorcycle and sidecar, Hubley Manufacturing Co., Lancaster, Pa., 1925 to 1935. Hubley made several motorcycle toys. This one is 9-1/2 inches long and costs $250 to $300.

Cast-iron vehicles, 6 inches to 12 inches long. Left to right: Crash Car motorcycle, Hubley Manufacturing Co., Lancaster, Pa., 1920 to 1930, $400 to $500; fire pumper, Kenton Hardware Co., Kenton, Ohio, 1910 to 1920, $125 to $160; coupe with rumble seat, A. C. Williams Co., Ravenna, Ohio, 1930 to 1935, $60 to $80.

Cast-iron vehicles, 7-1/2 inches to 13-1/2 inches long. Left: Coupe, Kenton Hardware Co., Kenton, Ohio, 1925 to 1930, $70 to $110. Right: Lincoln sedan and trailer, Hubley Manufacturing Co., Lancaster, Pa., 1938 to 1939, $85 to $130. Cars with attached trailers are somewhat rare.

Cast-iron bedroom set, Samuel Dowst Co., Chicago, 1930 to 1940. This firm also made complete kitchen, bathroom, living-room and even music-room sets. These toys, 2 inches to 3 inches high, were used to furnish dollhouses. This set is worth $40 to $65.

Painted cast-metal vehicles, some with plastic accessories, made by English manufacturers Corgi and Lesney, 1950 to 1975. These vehicles are 2-1/2 inches to 3 inches long. These readily available toys sell for $1 to $5 each. Their value will increase.

Three cast-metal and plastic warships, Samuel Dowst Co., Chicago, 1960 to 1970. These toys, 5 inches to 8 inches long, cost $4 to $8 each. Look for toy warships produced by Dowst from 1935 to 1940. These were all metal.

Sheet-steel toys. Left to right: Fire engine, 9-1/2 inches long, Wilkins & Kinsbury Manufacturing Co., Keene, N.H., 1920 to 1925, $75 to $125; clockwork-powered tractor, 8-1/2 inches long, Structo Manufacturing Co., Freeport, Ill., 1930 to 1935, $60 to $100; street sweeper, 7 inches long, Cragstan Co., Japan, 1950 to 1960, $45 to $60.

Modern sheet-steel toys. Left: Cement mixer, 15 inches long, Tonka Co., Japan, 1970 to 1975, $20 to $25. Right: Steamroller, 16-1/2 inches long, Nylint Toys, Rockford, Ill., 1970 to 1980, $15 to $25. These readily available vehicles eventually will be valuable collectibles.

Lithographed-tin registering banks, 1925 to 1950.
Left to right: Bank with black face, 7-1/2 inches
high, made in Germany, $100 to $135; Wheel of
Fortune, 8 inches high, manufacturer unknown, $70
to $90; children's registering bank, 4-1/2 inches
high, manufacturer unknown, $25 to $35; Punch &
Judy, 4-1/2 inches high, manufacturer unknown,
$75 to $90.

Wood and sheet-steel wheel toy, Keystone Manufacturing Co., Boston, 1935 to 1940. The child sat on the top and held the handlebars, which turned the front wheels. This toy is 31 inches long and costs $200 to $350.

Very detailed cast-metal farm equipment, 1950 to 1965. Left to right: Massey Ferguson combine, 7 inches long, Corgi, London; tractor and grader, 8 inches long, made by an unknown American manufacturer; backhoe, 4-1/2 inches long, Rodillo Co., West Germany. These toys sell for $10 to $20 each.

Solid-cast three-dimensional lead soldiers in various 18th- and 19th-century uniforms, Mignot Co., Paris, 1920 to 1935. These detailed soldiers are 2-1/2 inches high and cost $9 to $16 each. Mignot is one of the best-known French manufacturers.

Carved and painted wood rocking horse, made in the United States, 1910 to 1920. Factory-made 20th-century horses are not as valuable as earlier examples, but still bring substantial sums. This horse, 34 inches high, is worth $400 to $600.

Hollow-cast lead soldiers representing the Vatican Guard, Britains Ltd., London, 1950 to 1955. The Britains firm produced hundreds of different military miniatures. These examples are 2-1/2 inches high and sell for $8 to $12 each.

Early lithographed paper-on-wood toys are hard to find and expensive. Although it shows some wear, this locomotive costs $150 to $225.

Cast pot-metal cannons, made by several English and American manufacturers, 1950 to 1965. These cannons were 3 inches to 5 inches long, and were designed to accompany lead soldiers. These toys cost $7 to $15 each. Internal springs propel wood or metal projectiles.

Friction-powered locomotive made of painted wood and cast iron, Schieble Toy & Novelty Co., Dayton, Ohio, 1910 to 1925. This locomotive is 13 inches long and costs $90 to $155. You can assemble an interesting collection of friction toys.

Cast-iron locomotive, tender, boxcar, tanker and caboose, Kilgore Manufacturing Co., Westerville, Ohio, 1930 to 1935. Total length is 19 inches. Some enthusiasts collect freight trains, others collect passenger trains. This example costs $125 to $200.

Left: Puzzle-Peg, Lubbers & Bell Manufacturing Co., Clinton, Iowa, 1930 to 1935, $12 to $18. Center: Monopoly, Parker Bros., Salem, Mass., 1939 to 1950, $5 to $15. Right: Down and Out, Milton Bradley Co., Springfield, Mass., 1925 to 1935, $15 to $25. Because board games are plentiful and inexpensive, they are an excellent category for new collectors.

Left: Clockwork-powered locomotive, 5-1/2 inches long, made in the United States, 1920 to 1930, $350 to $400. Center and right: Tender and combined passenger-baggage car of tin plate, 4 inches and 6-1/2 inches long, Märklin Bros., Göppingen, Germany, 1925 to 1935. These examples sell for $75 to $100 each.

Roy Rogers horseshoe set, made in the United States, 1950 to 1960. This game has hard-vinyl horseshoes, and metal pegs and bases. It comes in a 10- by 18-inch box and costs $20 to $25.

Hard-plastic Lego construction toy, distributed by Lego Systems Inc., Enfield, Conn. about 1950 to 1970. Modern construction toys will be valuable collectibles in a few decades. This toy comes in a 12- by 20-inch cardboard box. It sells for $5 to $10.

Left: Lithographed tin-plate toy sink, 10-1/2 inches long, made in the United States, 1935 to 1940, $35 to $65. Right: sheet-steel and glass Modern Miss washing machine, 9-1/2 inches high, C. G. Wood Co., Girard, Pa., 1945 to 1950, $40 to $70. Similar toys include stoves, refrigerators, sets of kitchen cabinets and bathroom fixtures.

Cardboard gasoline station with lithographed
tin-plate gasoline pumps, Hull Toy Co., New York
City, 1925 to 1935. The set is 11 inches long and
costs $75 to $125.

Soft-plastic Smurf figures, made in Germany, 1975 to the present. The figures are 2 inches to 3 inches high. The buildings are 4 inches to 6 inches high. You can buy new Smurfs for about $2 to $3 apiece. Buildings and other accessories sell for $5 to $15. Smurfs are already being collected. The value of discontinued figures is increasing.

Battery-operated, radio-controlled, plastic-and-metal TRS 80 racing car, Radio Shack, New York City, 1970 to 1980. This car costs $25 to $50. It is 9-1/2 inches long.

Composition or papier-mâché nodding-head toys, made in Germany, 1935 to 1950.
Left to right: Donald Duck, 10-1/2 inches high, $85 to $115; small duck, 6 inches
high, $40 to $65; chick, 6 inches high, $30 to $50; Donald Duck bank, 6 inches high,
$60 to $80. The heads of nodding-head toys bob up and down because they are
connected to the bodies by springs.

Bibliography

This recommended list of books can help when you do toy research. Books marked with * are out of print and probably won't be readily available at bookstores. Books marked with † are privately printed or published by small, regional publishers. These too may be difficult to find. Therefore, you should supplement this list with books available from local libraries or used bookstores.

* Barenholtz, Bernard, and McClintock, Inez. *American Antique Toys, 1830-1900.* New York, N.Y.: Harry Abrams Inc., 1980.

* Bartholomew, Charles. *Mechanical Toys.* Secaucus, N.J.: Chartwell Books, 1979.

* Best, Charles W. *Cast Iron Toy Pistols, 1870-1940.* Englewood, Colo.: Rocky Mountain Arms and Antiques, 1973.

* Brown, George W. *The George Brown Toy Sketchbook.* Edited by Edith Barenholtz. Princeton, N.J.: Pyne Press, 1971.

* Buser, Elaine and Dan. *Guide to Schoenhut Dolls, Toys and Circus.* Paducah, KY.: Collector Books, 1976.

* Cadbury, Betty. *Playthings Past.* New York, N.Y.: Praeger Publishing, 1976.

* Chapuis, Droz. *Automata.* New York, N.Y.: Central Book Co., 1958.

* Culff, Robert. *The World of Toys!* New York, N.Y.: Hamlyn, 1969.

* Daiken, Leslie. *Children's Toys Throughout the Ages.* New York, N.Y.: Praeger Publishing, 1953.

* Foley, Daniel J. *Toys Through the Ages!* Philadelphia, Pa.: Chilton Co., 1962.

* Fraser, Antonia. *A History of Toys.* New York, N.Y.: Delacorte Press, 1966.

* Freeman, Ruth and Larry. *Cavalcade of Toys.* New York, N.Y.: Century House, 1942.

* Fritzsch, Karl Ewald, and Bachmann, Manfred. *Illustrated History of German Toys.* Translated by Ruth Michaelis Jena. New York, N.Y.: Hastings House Publishing, 1978.

* Grober, Karl. *Children's Toys of Bygone Days.* New York, N.Y.: Frederick Stokes, 1928.

* Harman, Kenny. *Comic Strip Toys.* Des Moines, Iowa: Wallace-Homestead Book Co., 1975.

* Hertz, Louis. *Handbook of Old American Toys.* Wethersfield, Conn.: Mark Haber, 1947.

* ———. *Mechanical Toy Banks.* Wethersfield, Conn.: Mark Haber, 1947.

* ———. *Messers Ives of Bridgeport.* Wethersfield, Conn.: Mark Haber, 1950.

* ———. *The Toy Collector.* New York, N.Y.: Funk & Wagnalls Inc., 1969.

* Hillier, Mary. *Pageant of Toys.* New York, N.Y.: Taplinger Publishing Co. Inc., 1966.

* Jendrick, Barbara Whitton. *A Picture Book of Paper Dolls and Paper Toys.* Pittsford, N.Y.: privately published, 1974.

Ketchum, William C., Jr. *Toys & Games.* Washington, D.C.: The Smithsonian Institution, 1981.

King, Constance Eileen. *The Encyclopedia of Toys.* New York, N.Y.: Crown Publishers, 1978.

* Lesser, Robert. *A Celebration of Comic Art and Memorabilia.* New York, N.Y.: Hawthorn Books, 1975.

† Long, Ernest and Ida. *Dictionary of Toys Sold in America, Vols. I and II.* Mokelumne Hill, Calif.: privately published, 1971 (Vol. I), 1978 (Vol. II).

* McClintock, Inez and Marshall. *Toys in America.* Washington, D.C.: Public Affairs Associates Inc. Press, 1961.

* McClinton, Katharine Morrison. *Antiques of American Childhood.* New York, N.Y.: Clarkson N. Potter Inc. 1970.

* McCollough, Albert. *The Complete Book of Buddy "L" Toys, A Greenberg Guide.* Sykesville, Md.: Greenberg Publishing Co., 1982.

* Meyer, John D., and Freeman, Larry. *Old Penny Banks.* Watkins Glen, N.Y.: Century House, 1960.

* Milet, Jacques, and Forbes, Robert. *Toy Boats 1870-1955.* New York, N.Y.: Charles Scribner's Sons, 1979.

* Moore, Andy and Susan. *The Penny Bank Book.* Exton, Pa.: Schiffer Publishing Co. Ltd., 1982.

* Munsey, Cecil. *Disneyana.* New York, N.Y.: Hawthorn Books, 1980.

Pressland, David. *The Art of the Tin Toy.* New York, N.Y.: Crown Publishers, 1976.

* Remise, Jac, and Fondin, Jean. *The Golden Age of Toys.* Greenwich, Conn.: New York Graphic Society, 1967.

* Rogers, Carole. *Penny Banks.* New York, N.Y.: E.P. Dutton, 1977.

Schiffer, Nancy, editor. *Matchbox Toys.* Exton, Pa.: Schiffer Publishing Co. Ltd., 1983.

* Spong, Neldred and Raymond. *Flywheel Powered Toys.* New York, N.Y.: Antique Toy Collectors of America, 1979.

* Weltens, A. *Mechanical Tin Toys in Color.* New York, N.Y.: Sterling Publishing Co. Inc., 1979.

* White, Gwen. *Antique Toys and Their Background.* New York, N.Y.: Arco, 1971.

* Whitton, Blair. *American Clockwork Toys 1860-1900.* Exton, Pa.: Schiffer Publishing Co. Ltd., 1979.

* Whitton, Blair, editor. *Bliss Toys and Doll Houses.* New York, N.Y.: Dover Publications, 1979.

Index